In the Company of Women

In the Company of Women:
100 Years at the Cosmopolitan Club

Historical Narrative by Lucienne S. Bloch

Edited by Sophia Duckworth Schachter, Caroline Fraser Zinsser, and Cynthia Van Allen Schaffner

The Cosmopolitan Club
New York City

Produced by the Centennial Book Committee

This centennial publication is a collaborative work begun over three years ago by members of the Archives Committee. Realizing the intensive work the project would entail, they formed a separate Centennial Book Committee and were joined by others. After much debate and reflection about what sort of history should be produced, committee members combined their talents in contributing to the overall production of the book—to the research, writing, editing, picture selection, scanning, and preliminary layouts. Christine Valentine graciously assumed the task of copyediting.

Lucienne Schupf Bloch
Damaris Smith Horan
Shelby M. Mamdani
Gail Hadley Rodney
Sophia Duckworth Schachter
Cynthia Van Allen Schaffner
Sandy Alcott Shalleck
Christine Valentine
Caroline Fraser Zinsser

Designed by Aaron Tilford and Ron Gordon of The Oliphant Press

Printed by Thames Printing in the United States of America

ISBN 978-0-615-24871-4

Cover illustrations: Renderings of the Club's facades by architect Thomas Harlan Ellett.

Contents

A Centennial Celebration—and Into the Future Molly O. Parkinson vii

A New Pegasus Caroline Fraser Zinsser ix

In the Company of Women Lucienne S. Bloch 1

The Cos in the Life of Its Members

Founders and Early Members Sophia Duckworth Schachter 71
The Cosmopolitan Club and the World of Education Evelyn J. Halpert 73
Five Decades Jill Ker Conway 74
Our Members in the Professions Charlotte P. Armstrong 76
A Clubhouse Fretted in Ironwork Cynthia Van Allen Schaffner 78
From Generation to Generation Ann Brewer Knox 80
The Cos Club, circa 1971 Lucy Schulte Danziger 81
Entertainments Esther Leeming Tuttle 82
Things My Mother Taught Me Rebecca Abrams 84
My Tea Susan Stevenson Borowitz 85
Macaroons and Cheese Soufflés Eleanor MacKenzie Graves 87
A Long Journey Marica Vilcek 88
The Arts in the Early Years at the Cos Club Wendy Jeffers 90
Reflections on Being a Member of the Cosmopolitan Club Tamara Kreinin 93
From Being "Ladies" to Being "Women" June Bingham 95

The Cos at 100, *photographs by Lindsay Brice* 98

Board of Governors 2008–2009 103

Former Presidents 105

Acknowledgments 107

Photography Credits 109

Diana, *a bronze statue, 1950, by Marion Sanford was given to the Club by Elisabeth Hamm.*

A Centennial Celebration—and Into the Future

As we celebrate and honor the centennial year of the Cosmopolitan Club, I am pleased to introduce this book by expressing thanks to all who have worked on it. The book committee that has so diligently researched and recorded the Club's history, both in words and images, has given us a treasure that will be enjoyed now and for years to come, and we are indebted to them for their stewardship and loyalty to our past. All who contributed are to be thanked as well for sharing their delightful and informative reflections.

Since the earliest days of our Club, members and leaders have addressed present realities while taking action to assure future needs. Programs consistently have reflected our members' efforts to understand current events and culture as well as their broad-minded embrace of the world. Our Club's survival can be attributed in large part to the drive to expand and renovate a succession of clubhouses and to keep up with the needs of the membership. Remarkable adaptability and creativity have enabled the Cos to thrive. It is our responsibility to assure that they remain hallmarks as we begin our second century. Our predecessors resisted the impulse to become hidebound. We honor that spirit!

While the women who went before us kept abreast of the many demands of the twentieth century, focusing in turns on the Great War, the Depression, World War II, and the bomb, among other major upheavals, they also had fun. Cos Club members allowed themselves the outlet of lighthearted entertainments. Their sense of humor is evident throughout the history you are about to read. They were accomplished in many realms, yet they never took themselves so seriously that they didn't occasionally take the risk of being silly and even raucous.

May our past inform us, and may our legacy be that we continue the efforts of all those who have made the Club the wonderful place that it is.

Molly O. Parkinson, President, Board of Governors

Right: Frances Grimes, creator of the Club bookplate. Below left: A new Pegasus emblem to celebrate our Centennial. Right: Our Pegasus bookplate, which dates from 1920.

A New Pegasus

In Greek mythology the immortal winged horse Pegasus was the offspring of Poseidon and Medusa. At the Cosmopolitan Club, Pegasus sprang from a convergence of literature, art, and classicism, and our rather curious habit of choosing clubhouse sites associated with stables. When the Club expanded its Fortieth Street quarters in 1917, there was room at last for a library. Among the first books to grace its shelves were the Oxford books of verse and translations of *The Iliad* and *The Odyssey*, all considered essential to the edification of Club members.

A new library called for a newly designed bookplate, and in 1920 one of the library's original supporters, Charlotte Hunnewell Sorchan, commissioned Frances Grimes, a noted sculptor and fellow member, to create one. The choice of Pegasus as its subject was made in recognition of his connection to the Muses, for it was the sacred spring formed by his hoof-print that gave the gift of song to all who drank from it. The complementary motto, *Vivida vis animi*, came from Lucretius and can be translated as "the lively force of the mind."

As Miss Grimes later recounted, "Although I studied many horses I did not find what I wanted until one day under a mounted policeman near Fifth Avenue, I saw what I had been looking for." She made an appointment to visit the stable, where she found several policemen eager to show off their horses' tricks. "Each horse was led out into an open space on the floor and made either to bow, shake hoofs, kneel or whinny in answer to a question. . . . Finally I was able to make studies of the horse which had so delighted me."

Since then Pegasus has served as both a noble and a beloved emblem of the Club, appearing in dignity on our official publications and more raffishly as a character in skits and at parties. For our centennial year, Pegasus is again reborn, this time prancing upward and forward into a new century, but with his foreleg touching the ground in homage to the sacred spring from whose waters flow inspiration for song and poetry and the arts and sciences.

CAROLINE FRASER ZINSSER

In the Company of Women

Lucienne S. Bloch

When an informal association for self-supporting women was started a century ago, its sponsors never imagined that it would become an important New York City institution treasured by generations of women with a wide range of talents, interests, professions, and groundbreaking accomplishments. Over the past one hundred years, the Cosmopolitan Club has been a home away from home for thousands of women who sought and found congenial companionship and intellectual excitement in a welcoming community. The Club changed in response to events in the world beyond its three clubhouses, but it always and unflappably maintained its original purpose: to offer hospitality and fun to serious women in a simple and unconventional gathering place. "Oh, bother the plumbing! Don't let us have plumbing, dear, let's have only charm!" exclaimed a member at a meeting about a proposed move to new quarters. The characteristic charm of the Cos was special and compelling, then and today.

The early history of the Club has been celebrated in anecdotal reminiscences by members on the occasions of its big anniversaries, at New Members Dinners, at theme parties and other events. Parts of the following narrative are taken from those inimitable reminiscences which, true to the formative spirit of the Club, were often presented as humorous skits, as songs and poems, in *tableaux vivants*, tap dances, and costume parades. Other parts are adapted from talks and written accounts, committee minutes and reports, and taped interviews with members. All of the primary source material is in the Club Archives, as are most of the illustrations. The overarching motif of these varied recollections is devotion to the Cos as a friendly haven for women. Unpredictable as life may be, it seems reasonable to believe that the Club's memorable past is prologue to its future.

Ethel Phelps Stokes Hoyt was concerned about the plight of a woman who worked for her. The Hoyt children's fräulein, Alice Kubler, mentioned to her employer that she had nowhere suitable to go on her days off. She had been meeting her friends and her brother on park benches, in the waiting room of the old and grimy Grand Central Depot, and in prohibitively expensive tea rooms and hotel lobbies. In the fall of 1907, Hoyt discussed the situation with Marion B. Langzettel, Principal of the Froebel League, a school on East

Facing page: Founder Adele Herter.

Left: Founder Ethel Phelps Stokes Hoyt. Right: Founder Edith Carpenter Macy. Below: The Cosmos Club brochure of 1909 brought in few members.

Sixtieth Street, and then enlisted the aid of Edith Carpenter Macy and Adele Herter. Together, the enterprising women came up with a plan. They would sponsor an informal social club for educated self-supporting women. And so it began.

An arrangement was made with the Froebel League, and for two years a group of teachers and governesses, most of whom were German, French, or British, met on week-ends in the League's classrooms. Alice Kubler led the club, which had about 30 members. Annual dues were an affordable sum of $5. Generous friends donated two wicker chairs and a tea set, which was for some months the entire equipment of the club.

In the spring of 1909, the sponsors decided on the name the Cosmos Club, to appoint Edith Macy President, and to move from the Froebel League to a rental apartment on East Thirty-third Street. These decisions mark the official birth of today's Cosmopolitan Club. In an effort to enlarge the membership so the Club could cover its new expenses, a circular describing the Cosmos Club was sent to city

President	*Vice-President*	*Treasurer*	*Secretary*
Mrs. V. Everit Macy	Mrs. Albert Herter	Mrs. John S. Hoyt	Miss E. Carse

THE COSMOS CLUB

142 East 33d Street

A Club for Governesses and Other Self-Supporting Women of Education

There is in America an ever-increasing demand for the best type of Governess—women of real refinement and high education who are able intelligently to co-operate with the parents in the mental, spiritual and physical nurture of the child. The position of governess, with its peculiar social isolation, has, heretofore, attracted but too few of the best type of educated women because of the scant opportunity it has afforded for recreation, discussion of common problems with fellow workers and other forms of development conducive to a higher efficiency.

Two years ago several young women holding positions as governesses formed a club and held meetings in a room loaned for the purpose by the Froebel League. These gatherings have been found so profitable and pleasurable that the members are eager to enlarge this Club and increase its possibilities. To this end they have enlisted the interest and co-operation of a number of women who have recognized the urgent need for such a Club.

It has been decided by the governesses and their co-operators that permanent quarters are essential for the success of this organization, which is fortunate in being able to begin its new year under the following conditions:

Through the generosity of one of the women interested, a large and charmingly furnished apartment has been secured on very favorable terms. There is a room for meetings, social and suburban women's schools and institutes and to settlement houses and libraries. That autumn, Elizabeth Carse, Headmistress of the Charlton School, became the Club President, and the name was changed to the Cosmopolitan Club for Women. The Club gave its first evening party on December 1, 1909, a soiree covered by the *New York Times*.

It soon became crystal clear that a club with a membership limited to self-supporting women paying minimal dues was a noble but unrealistic experiment. Moreover, the members weren't particularly keen on international sociability in an atmosphere of cultural uplift that ran to such events as a lecture about the tsetse fly and another on Japanese gardens. The governesses finally and tartly declared that it wasn't parties they wanted, but husbands.

Taken aback, the sponsors decided to go forward and reorganize the Club so that it could pay its own way with a mix of working women and financially comfortable members. The original idea of a club solely for professional and self-supporting women was definitively and permanently dropped. In April 1910, the Club's membership was officially opened to all women with an active interest in the arts, education, literature, philanthropy, and civic service. Annual dues were set at $10 for all members, and a Life Membership cost $250. With the help of Abby Aldrich Rockefeller, Josephine Pomeroy Hendrick, Helen Gilman Brown, Caroline McCormick Slade, and several other women, a different sort of club was launched.

gatherings, musicales, etc., and a number of bedrooms for members. The plan further provides a moderate priced restaurant and a bureau of information and employment, the privileges of which are available to all classes of members. The Superintendent engaged is a woman singularly fitted by experience and temperament to meet the various needs of her responsible position. She will act as resident matron, whose duties will include that of housekeeper, of confidential helper to those in trouble and need, and of agent between active members wishing positions and employer-members seeking governesses, tutors or secretaries.

As the ambition of the Club is to be self-supporting, it is eager to enroll as many new members as possible in order that the dues may cover expenses.

Life Members, $250.00 or more in any one year, are entitled to all the privileges of the various classes of membership.

Sustaining Members, annual dues $25.00 to $100.00, may introduce from one to four visitors a year according to the amount of annual dues, any one guest to remain for a period not to exceed two weeks.

Associate Members, annual dues $10.00, may introduce one visitor a year for a period not to exceed one week.

Active Members, annual dues $5.00, initiation fee $5.00. This membership is restricted to governesses, teachers and other self-supporting women who may be approved by the Committee on Admissions.

All members are entitled to the use of the Bureau of Employment without extra charge. Employers who are non-members may avail themselves of its privileges when introduced by a member of the Club and upon payment of a fee of $5.00 per year.

If you are in sympathy with the purpose of this Club, will you become a member by signifying upon the enclosed card the class of membership in which you wish to be enrolled?

Most women's organizations of the era focused on community improvement, literacy, the abolition of child labor, citizenship training and the Americanization of immigrants, better working conditions for women, and other equally vast issues. The founders of the Cosmopolitan Club were mindful of and involved with those concerns, but they had other ideas for their new club.

The founders' goal was a social club that would be much more than a lunchroom for busy women or a posh establishment where ladies of leisure could relax between bouts of shopping and symphony concerts. It would be an unpretentious meeting place where women could talk, listen, and learn, thereby expanding their contacts and knowledge of

The Dining Room of the Club when it was located in the Gibson Studio Building.

their community, their city and nation, and their global horizons. In the interest of emancipated inquiry, all shades of thought were welcome, but the Club would be distinctly nonpartisan. Professional women would make up at least one-third of the membership, and all the members should be, the Club's 1911 constitution stated, women "engaged in or interested in the liberal arts and professions." This was amended after World War I to include women "who have rendered public service." Above all, it would be a hospitable place for women seeking intellectual stimulation and entertainment. This intention was again emphasized in 1920 when the Club adopted its motto, from a poem by Lucretius: *Vivida vis animi*, the lively force of the mind. Then and still, that vital power sparks the Cos and its members.

From 1909 to 1913, the Club's headquarters were in the Gibson Studio Building at 142 East Thirty-third Street. Adele Herter lived in that building, as did Amey Aldrich, who promptly joined

Left: Amey Aldrich, author of Fifty Years Ago, *the Club history published in 1959.*
Right: Mary Schwarz as a horsefly in "A Party for Pegasus," 1951.

the Club "in self-defense," she later noted in a speech commemorating the Club's first fifty years that was published as a booklet in 1959 and subsequently given to all new members.

The Club's gaslit rooms were on the second floor, up a rickety stairway, and were modestly furnished with members' donations of chairs, china and cutlery, decorative items, and kitchen equipment. There was a dining room with ten small tables, a tiny kitchen, and several bedrooms, all of it overseen by a Superintendent, Mary Williams, who also ran an informal employment agency for teachers, secretaries, and governesses looking for work. She was assisted by Ellen, the cook-housekeeper, known as the Brigadier General. The lounge windows overlooked what a member called an "exstinkt" stable, although it was an active hack and livery yard. The buzz of horseflies was frequently heard during meetings, meals, receptions, lectures, and livelier diversions. The floors of the rooms were alarmingly wobbly, and two stout members agreed never to stand next to each other. The apartment was a firetrap; there was a metal pole outside one window for fast exits. Despite its drawbacks, the place was palpably delightful and much cherished by the early members. The finances of the Club were as shaky as its floors. The floors were propped up. The finances continued to sag. More members were needed to make the Club self-supporting.

A Membership Committee was formed, along with three other standing committees: House, Finance, and Arts and Interests, which had four subcommittees, Art, Music, Literature and Drama, and Public Interest. Members brought their friends to an increasing number of talks and concerts and evening parties at the Club in the hope of persuading them to join. The membership grew, slowly but surely.

By 1911, the Club was incorporated as the Women's Cosmopolitan Club. It had adopted its present constitution, held its first Annual Meeting, printed its first yearbook, and formed a wide range of committees responsible for the organization's governance, fiscal well-being, and programs. The issue of more space for the thriving Club had become a routine topic at meetings of the Board of Governors. There were now nearly 500 members. Dues had risen to $30 annually, or $500 for a Life Membership. There were fewer governesses but the same ratio of professional women to so-called general members. A lunch at the Club cost forty cents. Helen Brown was the first President of the

The Suffrage Parade of 1910 depicted in "The Days When a Woman Had Something to Fight For," 1950. Eleanor Edson is the flag bearer.

incorporated Club, which would be renamed the Cosmopolitan Club in 1915 when that corporate name became available in New York State. Members in that period included writers Willa Cather, Ellen Glasgow, and Ruth McEnery Stuart, actress Annie Russell, educator Maria Bowen Chapin, monologuist Ruth Draper, General Custer's widow Elizabeth Bacon Custer, violinist Katherine Parlow, journalist Ida Tarbell, sculptors Anna Hyatt Huntington and Mary Lawrence Tonetti, ballet dancer Adeline Genée, Grace Dodge, and other distinguished women, as well as a full complement of nonprofessional women who were effectively committed to cultural, civic, and political matters. Cos women marched in suffrage parades in New York City in 1909 and 1910 and were among the 8,000 women from every corner of America who marched on Washington, in March 1913, on the eve of President Woodrow Wilson's inauguration, to demonstrate for federal legislation granting women the right to vote. In 1950, the Club would give a party celebrating "The Days When a Woman Had Something to Fight For." One member in the pageant was carrying the dress she wore when she marched in 1913 because she had grown too plump to fit into it.

Members in costume for the first revel, "An Evening in a Persian Garden," 1913.

Cos members had a group talent for amusement in those early years and created their own entertainment, by no means amateurish. This inventive activity at the Club continued until the mid-1970s, when it became more difficult to find members with time to devote to Club theatricals and other festive presentations.

The first of many costume revels, "An Evening in a Persian Garden," was held in February 1913. There were members cavorting in ravishing costumes, snake dancers, and whirling dervishes, incense wafting from braziers, a crystal-ball seer, and a poet who declaimed Persian verses. Several members reported their concerns about unbecoming behavior at that party. A committee was appointed to investigate the complaint. Truly unacceptable or merely unusual, that evening was the talk of the town. Suddenly, large numbers of women were eager to join a club where such unique and exhilarating entertainment was presented by kindred spirits united in loyal and warm sociability.

The members' solidarity was tested by seismic rumbles of discontent about moving the Club from its homey quarters. After two years of heated debates and threats of secession if the Club relocated, the members reluctantly agreed that a larger clubhouse was needed to accommodate the increasing membership and program of activities. Committees were formed to look for a new building and to raise funds for a move that was, after all the stormy discussion, a triumph of necessity over nostalgia.

It certainly took imagination to see the possibilities in "a site of picturesque squalor," as a member called it, on the corner of Lexington Avenue at Fortieth Street. There were two old houses with adjoining backyards enhanced by two plane trees and a venerable wisteria vine. The adjacent building was a secularized Dutch Reformed church that had been converted to studios and apartments by its owners, Club member Mary Tonetti and her husband, François, both sculptors. The Tonettis frequently gave parties for such a variety of musicians, artists, thespians, writers, and dancers that the building was known as the *rive gauche* of Murray Hill. Encouraged by her neighbor on the same street, Club founding member Josephine Hendrick, Mary Tonetti urged the Club to consider the site. After the decision was made to rent the property, she was the presiding genius of the renovation of the houses that became the Club's headquarters, a structural ensemble that included the church's basement garage, formerly a stable.

The Board of Governors budgeted $40,000 for the move to Fortieth Street and work began on the transformation of seedy to enchanting. Naturally, it had to be done on a shoestring. Several architect husbands and relatives, including Charles A. Platt and Chester H. Aldrich, were summoned to the site to give their advice and views which, by and large, were discouraging. "Preposterous!" one architect called it. Plans for the renovation were made by an ingenious local builder, William Miller, and were presented to members at a special meeting in November 1912. After a scant year of demolition and excavation, of walls changing locations like gazelles bounding through space, all of it compounded by the predictable

The Reception Room of the expanded Fortieth Street Clubhouse, 1918.

difficulties and costly surprises of construction, the Cos had its new home.

On December 9, 1913, the Women's Cosmopolitan Club moved into its partly furnished headquarters. Fourteen days later, the Club gave a reception for Maria Montessori, an event presented in conjunction with the New York City Board of Education. The large Clubhouse had an assembly room, a lounge, a dining room, several meeting rooms, and a few bedrooms. The public rooms were furnished in Italian and Spanish taste and perhaps a somewhat antique discomfort; the private rooms were pleasant and cozier. Members contributed 113 decorative objects, including rugs, artworks, desks, tea sets, glassware, and pottery.

Musicales, plays, talks, readings, dances, displays of art by member Cecilia Beaux and of sculpture by Paul Manship soon followed that first year in the new building. There was now room for the art exhibits that would become a distinctive feature of the Club's program. Within the next three years, the Cos mounted exhibitions that included works by Monet, Renoir, Pissarro, Braque, Picabia, Picasso, Derain, Man Ray, Rivera, Joseph Stella, and other notable artists. The works were loaned by members or provided for sale by art dealers. When the Museum of Modern Art was born in 1929, its founders were three Cos members, Abby Aldrich Rockefeller, Lillie P. Bliss, and Mary Quinn Sullivan.

The Club had 600 members in 1914, some of them in the category of Nonresident, instituted two years earlier. The governesses had been teetering on the brink of extinction as members for the past few years, but there were many professional educators in the Club's membership. Headmistresses of New York City's schools and institutes for girls, along with women presidents of women's colleges, were usually proposed as members by alumnae of those institutions, and just about all of them readily joined the Cos, as they do today.

Lost & Found

The following articles have been found at the Club and will be disposed of unless claimed before March 1st.

Bag, beaded.
Cigarette case, leather.
Crepe square, brown.
Eye-glasses, ten pairs.
Gaiters, black.
Gloves, gray (new).
Gold brooch.
Gold stick pin.
Handkerchiefs.
Hat pins, two.
Japanese crepe, eight yards.
Neck piece, moleskin.
Purse, small green leather.
Purse, small pigskin.
Scarf, lace, two.
Scarf, Maribou.
Scarf, old rose silk.
Scarf, white chiffon.
Scarf, white silk.
Shawl, white.
Silk square.
Suit case, leather, containing clothing.
Sweater, knitted, yellow.
Veil, motor, black.
Veil, motor, brown.
Veil, motor, gray.
Vest, white linen, embroidered.
Walking sticks, three.

THE HOUSE COMMITTEE, 1914

In March 1914, the Club celebrated its move with a Roman revel. The evening was announced as a "Scenario from the Feast of Maecenas," and a costume committee was formed to advise members on authentic dress. Live goats were forcibly impelled down steps by scantily clothed bacchantes, noble Roman senators lolled on couches while slave girls in dishabille poured wine from amphorae, a spear carrier was helmeted with a jelly mold and wore a breastplate contrived of iron cooking pots and kettle cleaners, and songbirds in a large Lucullan pastry were released into the air and caught by the Tonetti children who kept them as pets. The sight of Anna Huntington doting on a wickedly handsome boy caused a flutter and an insistence that a male had been playing the boy's role in the spectacle. This was not the case. Men were welcome speakers and guests at Club events and dinners, but they would not act in the Club's theatrical presentations until 1952. Like the earlier Persian evening, the Roman revel's unbuttoned frolicking provoked some disapproval and disgruntlement among the members, one of whom complained that the goings-on showed too little respect for womanly dignity and reserve. Strictly conventional behavior and thought were not what made the Cos and its members tick, nor did conformity's starch stiffen its endearingly eccentric ambiance. Still, the prospect of reputation-smirching scandals was distressing. The Club revels that followed, and many did, were always quirky but definitely less risqué.

On December 13, 1914, the Literature Committee presented "Back of the Lines in Belgium," an evening with a speaker talking about his experiences, followed by a woman who read selections from war poems. World War I had begun four months earlier. Although President Wilson would not send American troops to the battlefields until April of 1917, after he tried and failed to resolve the conflict diplomatically, the European war and its military and civilian victims were on the minds of countless Americans and now figured prominently in the programming of the Club.

The Great War, so named in the erroneous belief that it would be the war to end all wars, lasted four cataclysmic years, during which Cos members responded actively in many ways. An Advisory War Committee oversaw the Club's efforts. Money was raised for Belgian relief

Above: During World War I, Bertha Coolidge, left, and Emily Cross, right, served in France in the Red Cross.

and for the purchase of an Italian ambulance. A war activity workroom was started and equipped with six knitting machines that produced hundreds of pairs of woolen socks every week which the Red Cross sent to soldiers in Europe. That particular war effort would be indelibly etched on the memory tablets of the Cos. In a 1933 speech, Helen Brown recalled a "picturesque moment when the Cosmopolitan Club Knitting Unit marched down Fifth Avenue as a part of the great Red Cross Parade [in May 1918]. It was divided into three squads, one composed of members winding wool, one engaged in knitting, and the third busily washing socks in shallow tin pans tied around the neck."

Over the years that the war lasted, talks were given at the Club on timely subjects. Among the lectures presented were "Nationality, Democracy and the War," "The Military Obligations of Citizenship," "Mobilization of Women for War Work," and "Internationalism." Lou Henry Hoover, Club member and future First Lady, spoke about the organized efforts of relief for war-torn Belgium. The now traditional and ever popular Tuesday Member Luncheons, the inspiration of Florence M. Marshall, head of the Manhattan Trade School, were started in February 1918 for the express purpose of presenting a member who would give a short account of the special public or emergency war work that she was doing. The first speaker was Delia West Marble, whose talk, "The Woman's Land Army," was heard following a lunch that cost sixty cents. The Club opened its ballroom to servicemen and nurses for dances, there were Cos members in uniform, an exhibit of French war posters, a concert held to raise money to buy wool for the knitters, readings of letters from soldiers and medical personnel in Europe, and many meetings at which members heard about and discussed ways that American women could participate in the international crisis by volunteering their services to organizations that dealt with medical needs, food, shelter, employment, and other issues that affected soldiers and civilians at home and abroad.

There was also fun in that period, one of the Club's idiosyncratic revels. In March 1916, the members regaled each other with "A Dutch Treat of ye XVII Century in ye renowned towne of New Amsterdam, being a Merrie Meeting of All Sorts and Conditions of Men, Women and Children and Various Kindly and Curious Creatures." For that evening, the Ballroom was transformed into a square in old New Amsterdam. Mary Tonetti was a doughty pirate stranded on a foreign shore where she and her crew were overpowered by local Indians and were rescued in the nick of time by two strolling players, Annie Russell

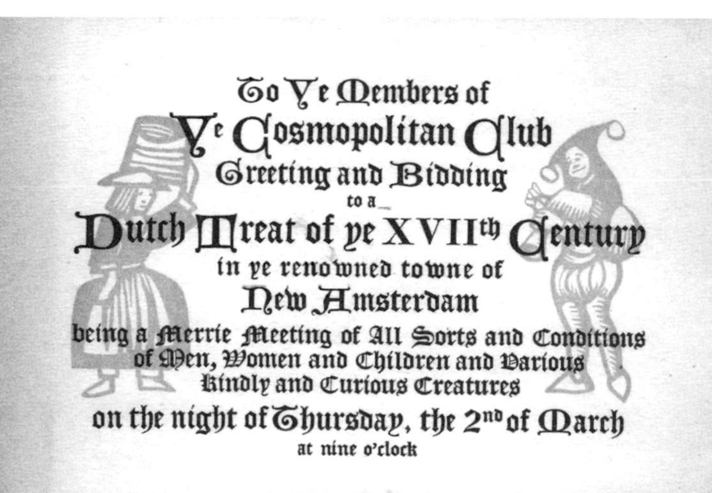
To Ye Members of
Ye Cosmopolitan Club
Greeting and Bidding
to a
Dutch Treat of ye XVIIth Century
in ye renowned towne of
New Amsterdam
being a Merrie Meeting of All Sorts and Conditions
of Men, Women and Children and Various
Kindly and Curious Creatures
on the night of Thursday, the 2nd of March
at nine o'clock

THE ARTS AND INTERESTS COMMITTEES

have arranged a series of very informal buffet luncheons to be held in the Assembly Room on successive Tuesdays, beginning February 19th, from one to two o'clock.

At each luncheon some member of the club will give a short account of the special public or emergency war work in which she is engaged, thus affording an opportunity to learn of the different activities represented in our membership.

Four of these meetings have been planned and should the response warrant their continuance, the Committees are prepared to carry them through the season. It has been decided to limit the attendance, for the present, to members only, in order that the general discussion may be quite informal.

The price of the luncheon will be 60 cents and checks should be signed before entering the Assembly Room.

In order that the House Committee may cater to the best advantage, members are requested to signify their intention of attending the luncheon not later than the preceding Monday.

The speaker will be introduced each day at 1.45 and, if possible, she will remain beyond the hour, to answer any questions which the members may wish to ask in connection with her work.

ON TUESDAY, FEBRUARY 19TH

MISS DELIA MARBLE

WILL SPEAK OF

THE WOMAN'S LAND ARMY

TUESDAY, FEBRUARY 26TH

MISS AMEY ALDRICH

WILL SPEAK OF

PROTECTION OF WOMEN IN NEW INDUSTRIES

The speakers for the other dates will be posted on the bulletin board and, when possible, notices will be enclosed with other mailed matter.

Announcement of the first Members Luncheons, 1918.

and Edith Wynne Mathison, who subdued the natives with the sweet words of the balcony scene from *Romeo and Juliet*. It is easy to imagine the glee produced by that zany skit performed in a manner that redefined farcical.

March 1st to 20th

Five Paintings

Lent by

MRS. SAMUEL A. LEWISOHN

Will be Exhibited in the Lounge

"WOMAN IN BLUE"..........PABLO PICASSO

"GIRL IN SPANISH SHAWL"..........HENRI MATISSE

"THREE WOMEN"..........PAUL GAUGUIN

A FLOWER PICTURE..........ODILON REDON

HEAD OF A SMALL GIRL..........MODIGLIANI

1920

Entertainment was only a small part of the Club's activities while the war raged. The relief efforts and war-driven programs continued to occupy the thoughts, hearts, and hands of the members, but pressing issues arose within the Club. In the fall of 1916, the Cos was confronted with a strike. The staff was demanding higher wages, shorter hours, and less work. After arbitration, the demands were met, but with the unavoidable outcome of increased restaurant charges and, subsequently, higher dues. Over the years, the Cos would generally be sympathetic to the welfare of its staff, not surprising in an organization originally established for self-supporting women.

Another concern was the enlargement of the Clubhouse. A questionnaire was sent to members in the summer of 1916 to survey their views on expanding into two more houses on Lexington Avenue. The response was resoundingly favorable, and the houses were bought by Laura Billings Lee, then the Club President. She and ten other members formed a holding company, Cosmos Realty, which leased the two buildings to the Club at a reasonable cost.

Edward C. Dean was chosen as the architect for the expanded Clubhouse, which opened on November 5, 1917. The Cos now had a larger dining room, a library, more meeting rooms and bedrooms, more space for events and art exhibits. Stairways connected the several levels of the combined buildings. An arcaded loggia led to a flagstone terraced patio, a new feature of the Clubhouse. The building's main rooms and corridors were oriented to the gracious and quite romantic Sicilianesque inner patio, which had rosy brick walls, attractive plantings, and a member-donated marble fountain with a sculpted frieze; that fountain can be seen today near the entrance to the Lounge.

Yet another serious note was sounded in 1917: the Club's view of its patriotic duties. A resolution was adopted at the Annual Meeting in April that read: "We, the members of the Cosmopolitan Club . . . shall hereby pledge to our country the utmost service of which we are capable in thought, word and deed . . . that we may contribute our part to the realization of that ideal of which we dream, which is America." This resolution has undertones of a loy-

The interior courtyard of the Fortieth Street Clubhouse, 1918.

alty oath, implicit if unsworn.

The issue of patriotic loyalty would rise to the surface two years later during a nationwide Bolshevist-Socialist scare prompted by the Russian Revolution. More than twenty members protested in a letter to the Board of Governors that the Club was being used as a public forum for un-American political gatherings and purposes, potentially tainting the Cos and its members. In a response dated November 19, 1919, that was circulated to the entire membership, the Governors took the "opportunity to review the policies and character of the Club in past years and to recall . . . those qualities which have contributed most directly to its vitality and its hold on the interest and affection of the members. The Cosmopolitan Club was organized for purposes of entertainment, social intercourse and the interchange of opinion among women of artistic and intellectual interests. . . . The Governors believe that a tradition of intellectual hospitality was then definitely established, but with equal definiteness a tradition of nonpartisanship. The Club does not endorse, defend or attack the opinions expressed by its guests and its speakers. It welcomes the significant voices of the day in art, literature and public affairs, but it exists as a social club for the benefit of its members." Despite this strong statement by the Board of Governors, the controversy about the use of the Club lasted another year.

Noted Speakers and Performers *1915–1931*

Jacinto Benavente
Walter de la Mare
Robert Frost
John Galsworthy
Dubose Heywood
Julian Huxley
Rockwell Kent
Thomas W. Lamont
Vachel Lindsay
Amy Lowell
Luigi Pirandello
A Delegation of Pueblo Indians
Dora Russell
Carl Sandburg
Siegfried Sassoon
Konstantin Stanislavski
Rear Admiral Charles H. Stockton

The Club's traditional policy went beyond ideological tolerance. Although many Cos members were sincerely tickled by the fact that it never was and was never publicly seen as a fashionable club for high society ladies of leisure, another fact is that many of the early members had impeccable credentials identifying them as women who belonged by birth or marriage to America's upper crust. Even so, broad-mindedness trumped elitism at the Cosmopolitan Club; its very name speaks for its unprovincial intentions. The Club had international members in its earliest incarnation as a meeting place for governesses, and it was always socially unhidebound, welcoming members who needed to work for a living.

After World War I ended, women turned to other battles. There was a new order of things to understand and, for the Club's activists, to tackle—new domestic and foreign policies to learn about, more educational and professional opportunities for women, advances in medicine and science, and avant-garde art and music and literature to puzzle over and maybe admire. Between 1919 and 1932, Cos members heard talks on a broad spectrum of postwar isms: pacifism, Freudianism, spiritual eclecticism, thrill-seeking sensationalism, pluralistic idealism, modernism, consumer materialism, and other subjects requiring the thoughtful attention they got from Cos audiences. The programs were well received, though sometimes a bone of contention. When birth control was proposed as a lecture topic in 1926, there was opposition from some of the more cautious members. "Let there be light!" a pluckier member declared, resolving the dispute. Cos members heard the lecture, and the sky didn't fall.

Eminent members' talks at the Club in that period were Eleanor Roosevelt's "What Democratic Women Want," and "Unemployment Today and Tomorrow," presented by Frances Perkins. Journalist Dorothy Thompson spoke on the

A Three Dimensional, Unsolvable, Non-interlocking Puzzle

Announcing

The FOOLS' PARTY

For Members Only

At the Cosmopolitan Club on April 1st, at nine o'clock

HORIZONTAL

1. Date of the Members' Party, the Cosmopolitan Follies.
2. Hour that the Vaudeville Performance will begin in the Assembly Room. Bill to consist of Startling turns by Members Only.
3. Object of Mammoth Party for Members. Two entire floors to be thrown open for April Fool's Day Frolic.
4. Horoscope reading in the Cave of the Occult.
5. Palmistry by a Wizard of the West, as well as other weird and delightful surprises at every turn.

VERTICAL

6. Entertainment all the evening, upstairs and down by that which hath charms to sooth the savage breast.
7. Something to see and to indulge in.
8. No wine, but plenty of the other two.
9. That which will be served upstairs after the Great Show and is included in the General Admission charge of $1.50.
10. All Members adjured to come in costume to the Cosmopolitan Follies on Wednesday, April 1st, at nine o'clock.

CIRCULAR

A. Costumes, appropriate or inappropriate, required.

B. Come as a Jester, Clown, Court Fool or Punch. See suggestions enclosed.

C. Historical and Literary Fools welcomed. All kinds admitted.

D. Paper fools-cap and scarf will pass muster. Any and every costume is O.K.

Admission, including Vaudeville, Music, Side Shows, Dancing, Supper, Etc., $1.50

PLEASE NOTIFY THE OFFICE THAT YOU ARE COMING

Committee on Arts and Interests
MRS. CLARENCE BISHOP SMITH
Chairman

The invitation to "The Fools Party," 1925, a year when crosswords were all the rage.

revolutionary process in Germany.

THURSDAY, FEBRUARY NINTH
At 8:45 P. M.

Dora Russell
writer, lecturer and educator, actively interested in The Labor Party and the Birth Control Movement in England, who conducts with her husband, The Hon. Bertrand Russell, a modern experimental school for children at Petersfield, in Sussex

Author of "*Hypatica*" and "*The Right to be Happy*"
will speak on

The Moral Outlook of the Modern
1928

The new Clubhouse had been looking a tad shabby since 1919, understandably, as there were now nearly 800 members passing through it frequently and a sizable increase of events presented in its public rooms. Funds for the building's necessary repairs and improvements were raised by a members' assessment of $10 and by contributions. The much-used Assembly Room was slated for major refurbishment. The Club commissioned mural painter Allyn Cox to redecorate that room. When his work was finally unveiled in 1923, it raised the hackles of several squeamish and vocal members. "A navel and umbilical cord parade!" one of them harrumphed. "There really isn't a room in this building where one can take a clergyman," complained another. Cox had painted almost completely naked caryatids on the pilasters. There was talk of covering his work with curtains, but this was wisely voted down. The dazzling though perhaps ungenteel art remained visible to members and their guests until the Club moved to its present location nine years later. In 1936, Cox would paint the grisaille panels in today's Main Dining Room, works that represent the Club's interest in the arts, literature, and science.

The Club gave its first postwar revel in April 1921, a "Spanish Party" that was a glamorous evening of Castilian beauties dancing to the click of castanets and otherwise disporting themselves for a highly appreciative audience. That same month, members contributed over $4,000, a hefty sum in those days, to the Herbert Hoover Relief Fund for Polish Children. This duality of purpose was a hallmark of the Cos: gravitas and amusement, both genuine, distinct but counterbalanced. For today's members in today's world, the scale tips toward serious-mindedness.

Another of the Club's now legendary revels took place in March 1922, a mid-Victorian party billed as "An Informal Rout with Scenes from the Life of Our Dear Queen." There was a pageant of members in period clothing, during which the audience witnessed the wooing of Albert, the welcome of five royal offspring, admired the noted photographer Alice Boughton posing as the beautiful queen depicted in Thomas Sully's portrait, heard bagpipes

The semi-naked caryatids of the decoration designed by Allyn Cox for the Assembly Room caused a stir in 1923.

skirl and songs beloved of their grandmothers, and as a finale saw the elderly monarch unveiling the Albert Memorial. That evening seems more like a sentimental journey to a lost world than a boisterously jolly rout. Either one, it was thoroughly enjoyed.

American women had won the right to vote in 1920, and there was little if any nostalgic retrospection about the lost pre-suffrage world. On the contrary, that victory gave women a green light to make the changes they could. Social and marital formality declined, skirts and hair were shortened, simpler food was put on family tables, women had more to say in the management of their finances and were more effective in political arenas. Many other changes advanced women's independence in the post–World War I period, as would happen again after World War II, all of them steps on the bumpy, twisty road that led to a full-bore women's liberation movement in later years.

A self-portrait of photographer Alice Boughton who was portraying Queen Victoria in the "Mid-Victorian Party," 1922.

The Twenties were also the Jazz Age. It arrived with an exuberant roar after the war ended and was proceeding at a heady and hedonistic pace, only marginally cramped by legislation that enforced Prohibition throughout the United States in 1920. In comic skits that were performed at the Club's "Flaming Youth Party" in 1930 and its "Coming of Age" celebration in 1932, older members were affectionately spoofed as wets, suggesting that liquid refreshment in handy pocketbook flasks was tippled at the Club throughout Prohibition, which wasn't repealed until 1933. "The Old Bloods know how to live, they have fun! They don't have to be the backbone of the nation, they're through with that!" a Young Blood said in a skit written by Marya Mannes in what she called "a weak moment."

When mother was a little girl,
She used to speak politely,
She never was allowed to act,
The very least bit sprightly.

Then she joined a woman's club,
And started making whoopee,
Now she's at the club all day,
Poor ma is changed completely!

Mother, mother, tut, tut, tut,
Can you expect your daughter,
When you are at a club all day,
To do the things she oughter?

Sung at the "Flaming Youth Party," 1930,
to the tune of "Yankee Doodle"

There were plenty of dry, but never dull, events at the Cos during those years. There was so much happening at the Club that the *Broadside*, today's *Bulletin*, was started in 1931 to inform members about the programs and give them Club news.

The Cos was outgrowing its garage and neighboring houses as it outgrew the apartment above the stable on Thirty-third Street and had begun to think about moving again. A Ways and Means Committee was formed in 1928 to investigate the possibility of a new clubhouse. The leases on the Fortieth Street houses would expire in 1932 and would have to be renewed at greater cost if the Club stayed put. There were now more than 1,000 members, who paid annual dues of $60. More members were needed to defray the Club's expenses. A bigger membership required bigger quarters. Given those givens, a move was inevitable.

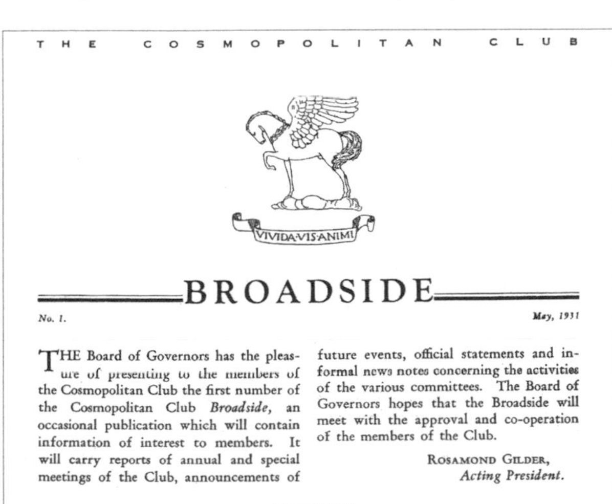
THE COSMOPOLITAN CLUB

VIVIDA VIS ANIMI

BROADSIDE

No. 1. May, 1931

THE Board of Governors has the pleasure of presenting to the members of the Cosmopolitan Club the first number of the Cosmopolitan Club *Broadside*, an occasional publication which will contain information of interest to members. It will carry reports of annual and special meetings of the Club, announcements of future events, official statements and informal news notes concerning the activities of the various committees. The Board of Governors hopes that the Broadside will meet with the approval and co-operation of the members of the Club.

Rosamond Gilder,
Acting President.

Broadside, *the Club's first bulletin, was launched in May 1931.*

FOR SALE OR RENT
FRED'K FOX & CO.
EVES
DANIEL REEVES
3446 - 3.7.32
122 E. 66 ST. N.Y.C.

A special meeting of the Cosmopolitan Club was held on April 28, 1930. Approximately 225 members heard a summary report from the Ways and Means Committee, chaired by Anne Kidder Wilson. The committee had previously given the Board of Governors a full report of its work and its well-informed recommendations, along with a sketch by an architect showing how the proposed properties at 122–124 East Sixty-sixth Street and 129 East Sixty-fifth Street could be combined to provide the space and facilities needed. Those properties had recently come on the market and were bought and held for the Club by Laura Lee, often called the fairy godmother of the Cos. Almost predictably, there was a stable on one of the sites. Over the past two years, the committee had looked at 160 possible locations, most of them north of the midtown area the Club had been in for seventeen years. The quiet allure of Lexington Avenue at Fortieth Street had vanished, giving way to noisy skyscraper construction and the bustle and congestion of a thriving business district; several other social clubs had already moved to the Upper East Side's more residential neighborhoods.

Despite the stock market crash in October 1929 and the dismal financial picture it painted overnight, the committee recommended that the Club should own property, not lease it as they had been doing, and further recommended that the Club buy the sites from Laura Lee and build a new clubhouse. The price of the two properties was a reasonable $305,000. The estimated cost for a new building was $455,000, which included professional fees, liability insurance, and a cushion for unforeseen expenses. The neighborhood was suitably uncommercial and likely to stay that way, the character of the block was protected by its private houses with rear gardens, its studio buildings, and by the historic and architecturally impressive Seventh Regiment Armory. The Sixty-sixth Street site had good southern light that could be ensured by the purchase of the brownstone on Sixty-fifth Street. The location was convenient to public transportation on Lexington Avenue and not far from Grand Central Terminal, used by many Nonresident Members when they traveled to the Club. After all of these strong points were presented at the meeting, a motion to authorize the Governors to act on the committee's recommendations was made, seconded, and carried unanimously. Further meetings were scheduled to discuss financing the project, always a complex undertaking, more so in ruinous economic times.

Facing page: The new Clubhouse under construction, 1932. Above: The Havemeyer stable, center, that occupied the site of the Sixty-sixth Street Clubhouse.

Friday Afternoon Conferences on the Present Economic Situation and Unemployment at 4:15 p. m.

JANUARY 16TH.	Mr. Rexford G. Tugwell of the Department of Economics of Columbia University will speak of "The Economist's View of the Present Situation."
JANUARY 23RD.	Miss Beulah Amidon, Editor of the Survey Graphic, will speak of "Seasonal Unemployment."
JANUARY 30TH.	Miss Frances Perkins, Industrial Commissioner, Department of Labor, State of New York, will speak of "Constructive Measures to Avoid Unemployment Crises."
FEBRUARY 6TH.	Miss Mary Van Kleek, Director of Industrial Studies, Russell Sage Foundation, will speak of "The World as a Unit."

1931

Before detailed architectural plans were made, a questionnaire was sent to members asking how they might use the new building socially and what they would like to have in it; athletic facilities, a permanent stage for theatricals, a hairdressing salon, an exhibition gallery, and a ticket agency were some of the amenities listed on the questionnaire. Responses poured in, 531 in all, so many and so diverse that Eleanor Hardy Platt, Chair of the Building Committee, despaired, saying she felt "like St. Ursula on her deathbed, dying not of mortal disease but of the contest of many minds." Legend has it that St. Ursula was accompanied to her martyrdom by 11,000 maidens; 1,047 Club minds reached a consensus about the new building: informal, unconventional, aesthetically pleasing, a place that would reflect a spirit of friendship and a vital interest in the liberal arts: the tried-and-true model of a Cos clubhouse.

Then came the hard part. Against formidable odds in the thick of a deep worldwide Depression and the hardships it imposed on millions of people, many Cos members, staff and their families included, the Club succeeded in raising the astonishing sum of $885,000. The Finance Committee, chaired by Fanny Hastings Plimpton, worked with undaunted courage and epic resolve to secure the necessary funds. They framed and then implemented a five-year fiscal plan based on several factors, the primary one being the expansion of membership to 1,450 over two years. Dues would rise to $85 and a modest assessment of $15 would be made. A mortgage would be obtained from a dependably solid bank. This mortgage was later said to have been so cleverly negotiated by a member that the Club got it without a fee. A five-year debenture bond of $400,000 would be issued and sold to members; by 1946, more than half that bond would be redeemed and the Cos would pay off its first mortgage, prompting a gentleman banker to remark in amazement: "What a club, what a club."

An important though unwritten part of the five-year plan was the customary generosity of members devoted to the Cos. The August 1931 *Broadside*, in its Heard in the Members Dining Room column, reported a youngish woman saying, "I don't think we can possibly build until this Depression is over, but I've sent in my pledge so they know they can count on that little bit."

The little bits added up.

Demolition of the stable on Sixty-sixth Street began in November 1931. After considering a number of noted architects, the Building Committee selected Thomas Harlan Ellett and hired Walter D. Binger as the construction engineer, both married to Cos women and fathers of future members. The cornerstone of the Clubhouse was laid on May 19, 1932, by Club President Alida Leese Milliken. The week before, the Club gave its last party on Fortieth Street. It was a "Coming of Age" celebration, then counted from the Club's incorporation in 1911, now fixed as 1909 for the Club's actual start. That evening, former Club President Helen Brown read her comic verses about the life and journeys of Pegasus, by then the Club's emblem. There were also skits performed at that party, one of them titled "Moving Becomes the Cos Club." Better than mourning, for sure.

The construction progressed at lightning speed, stopped only by a seven-week builders' strike in the summer of 1932. On November 19, 1932, exactly one year from the day demolition began, the Cos officially moved into its new and present home. A tea was given that afternoon for members who wished to see the completed and furnished building. Ellett and Binger were on the landing at the top of the stairs in the front hall, tending to last-minute problems. When the doors opened at four p.m., Ellett looked down and reportedly said to Binger, "Good God, Walter, what are all those women doing here!"

Ellett's design for the Club building is both modern and classical in its simplicity of form and material, and was deliberately different from the elaborate Beaux Arts or the severer Italianate Renaissance styles that were the look of choice for most urban social clubs and many palatial residences built by the city's wealthy. The original and ongoing culture of the Cos doesn't encourage stately or showy, as the restrained elegance of its Clubhouse demonstrates. In 1933, Ellett was awarded the Gold Medal of the Architectural League of New York for his design of the Cosmopolitan Club.

The ten-story Clubhouse has had no major structural changes since it opened seventy-seven years ago. The usage of some rooms has changed. A small bedroom on the fifth floor became a computer room for members' use while in the Club. There was a hairdressing salon on the ninth floor from 1935 to the mid-1980s, a popular convenience for members and their daughters; that space is now occupied by the business office. The Sixty-fifth Street building formerly housed a squash court with a viewing gallery and dressing rooms; today it is used as an exercise studio and for storage space. Other times, other demands. The beauty

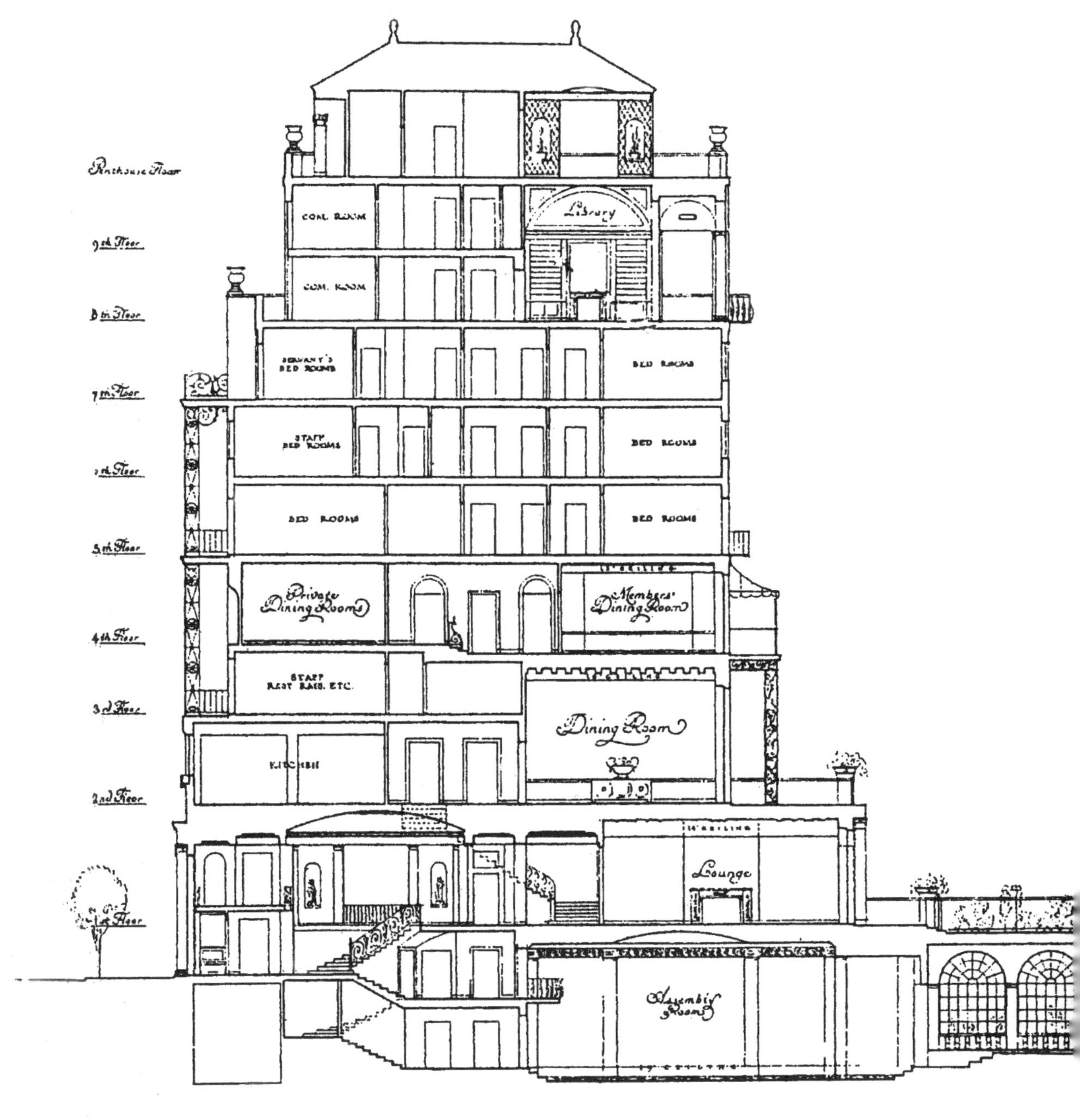

LONGITUDINAL SECTION

parlor is gone, the computers are here.

The Clubhouse's handsome entrance hall on Sixty-sixth Street with its paired curving stairways, the Lounge, double-height Library, top-floor Sun Room, dining rooms, Ballroom, terraces, bedrooms, and inner courtyard are essentially as they were when the building opened; their decor has changed over the decades due to wear and tear and taste, but their Thirties bones remain, though buried in places. The fourth-floor Private Dining Room was first decorated by members Claire Kennard and Constance Ripley; the rest of the Clubhouse was the work of Eleanor McMillen, founder of McMillen Inc. The Club's interiors were featured in many magazines, among them *American Architect, Town & Country, House and Garden,* and *House Beautiful.* The well-known photographer Samuel Gottscho took pictures for several of those articles. Prints of his work are in the Club Archives, along with other photographs depicting the rooms as they once looked. There are photographs of the bold abstract murals by Charles H. Howard in the Private Dining Room and of the scroll-backed Regency-style chairs he designed for that room. Each chair has a slightly different needlepoint seat cover, all made "over half the globe by members summering on at least two continents," a *Broadside* reported. Julia Isham Taylor, Chair of the House Committee, donated funds for the decoration of the Sun Room on the tenth floor. Two artists were invited to submit their designs for a mural, which should depict the courtyard of the Club's Fortieth Street building. Henrik Mayer, a Yale Art School graduate, was chosen. Unfortunately, the photographs of his artwork are badly faded, and the mural itself disappeared when the Sun Room was redecorated in 1959.

The Library Committee had organized an exhibit in the previous Clubhouse, in February 1931, displaying 220 books written, illustrated, designed, or bound by members. Now the committee worked with the Art, Drama, and Music Committees to compile basic bibliogra-

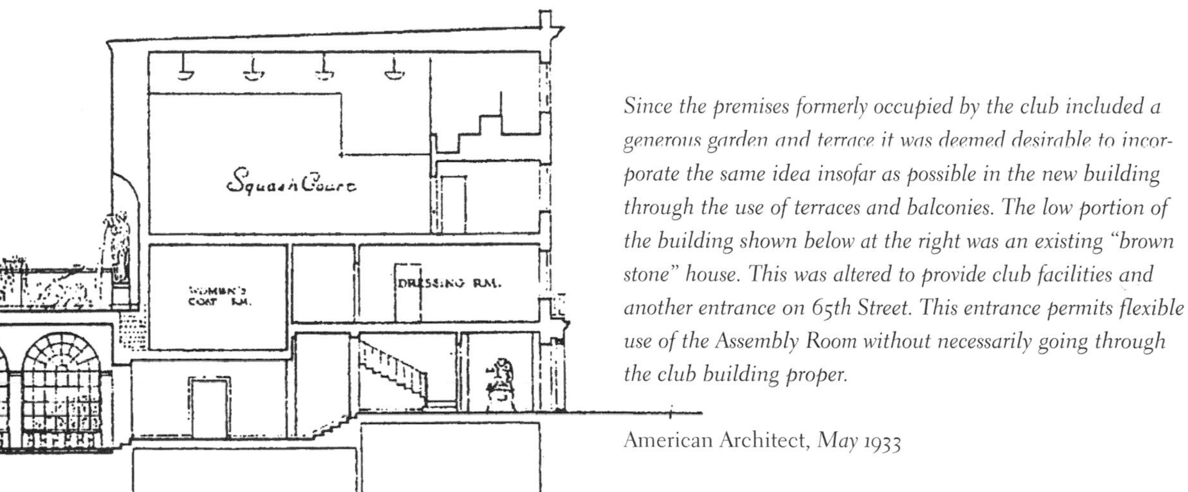

Since the premises formerly occupied by the club included a generous garden and terrace it was deemed desirable to incorporate the same idea insofar as possible in the new building through the use of terraces and balconies. The low portion of the building shown below at the right was an existing "brown stone" house. This was altered to provide club facilities and another entrance on 65th Street. This entrance permits flexible use of the Assembly Room without necessarily going through the club building proper.

American Architect, *May 1933*

Left: The Private Dining Room after its decoration by members Claire Kennard and Constance Ripley. This is one of the many photographs of the interior taken in 1933 by Samuel H. Gottscho. The chairs of the Private Dining Room designed by Charles H. Howard had needlepoint seat covers stitched by Club members.

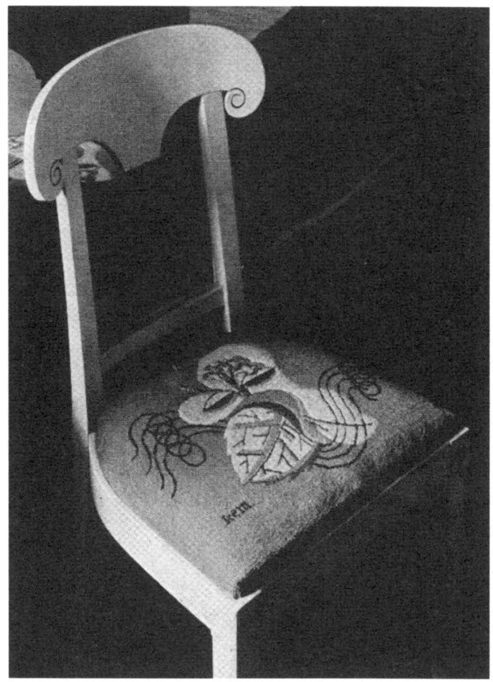

phies in those fields, adding reference lists in philosophy, science, and economics. The Library Committee formulated a book-buying plan that would make the contents of its shelves worthy of its beautiful new room. The Cos Library is still exceptionally attractive and has more than 4,000 books in its collection, of which about 1,400 are by members, although not every book by members is in the collection. In 1940, the Club would start a special collection of theater-related material as a memorial tribute to Maud Durbin Skinner, an actress and former Club President. In 1954, the Skinner Collection was moved from the Library into a newly created Members Room on the eighth floor.

An inaugural party for the Clubhouse was held on February 9, 1933. The Cos resumed its usual and full schedule of eclectic events: informative lectures, concerts, revels, art exhibits, dances, receptions, theatrical performances, and more. Squash games and tournaments were

The Library, decorated by McMillen Inc., as it looked in 1933.

new activities at the Club, and male guests playing with members could use the court in the evenings and on weekends; the Club was open on weekends from its beginnings until 1976. Other innovations were a members' choral group led by Margarete Dessoff, a small orchestra composed of musician members, and a thirty-session exercise course described as "a system [that] aims at the evolution of a perfectly conditioned body, the overcoming of tension and resultant fatigue, and the building up of reserve vitality in the course of which graceful carriage and graceful curves result." There were also classes in folk dancing and bridge.

Soon after the Cos settled into its new building, a decision was made to form an Archives

Margot Morrow and Mary Villard, squash rackets in hand, in a skit presented at the New Members Dinner of 1952.

Committee, which was chaired by Rosamond Gilder, then the Club President. In response to a request made a few years before, members had been handing in material about the Club's early years, and this was organized and filed or pasted into scrapbooks. The Archives Committee has continued to collect reports, records, letters, photographs, reminiscences, memorabilia, publications, and newspaper and magazine clippings about members or about the Club; oral histories began in 1985, and those tapes were added to the archives. The archival material was at first kept in the Members Room that was later divided into today's Skinner Room and Archives Room.

In April 1936, the Club gave itself a twenty-fifth anniversary party, still reckoned from 1911. Costumes were obligatory and had to represent the period from 1910 to 1914. Anne Tonetti Gugler described the celebration in a letter to her mother, Mary. "It was priceless," Gugler wrote, "all the Presidents [of the Club] were there, everyone in 1911 costumes except for the Old Guard who were in French soldiers' uniforms." Nathalie Dana played the part of Brigadier General Ellen, the housekeeper at the Club's first home on Thirty-third Street.

Entertainment apart, there were somber programs in those years, focused on problems facing the world: the continuing Depression for one, the swift and ominous rise of Hitler for another.

The Club was part of an effort started by a private group in New York, an Emergency Unemployment Relief Committee to assist out-of-work New Yorkers. There was an Adopt-a-Family drive to which Cos members donated more than $2,000, the largest amount given by an independent club in New York City; $40 of that sum was contributed by Club employees, who surely couldn't afford it but gave anyhow. The

Pegasus outside the Archives Room, a memorial tribute of 1995 by Meredith Hamilton to Wynne Fooshee, Club Archivist, 1973 to 1989.

BROADSIDE

NET INCOME, LIQUOR 1,313.42

$ 400,000 A PLEA

FANNY HASTINGS PLIMPTON,
Chairman, Finance Committee

We have had an excellent year.

AGNES B. LEACH,
President

9 8 5

66TH STREET BONDS

BONDHOLDERS 1911 - 1936

10% Government Tax on above $10

SQUASH COURT

"Man the Unknown"

65TH STREET PLAN

6 7 LOCKERS

FIVE YEAR PLAN

KITCHENS

NET INCOME, CIGARS $0

Board of Governors SINKS

SUNROOM FOR SUN BATHING

HOUSE COMMITTEE

1 2 3

BUY LIBRARY BONDS

for Members Only

Twenty-fifth Anniversary

The total $ indebtedness of the Club

10 MORTGAGES

$ 353,000 House Charges

CURRENT LIABILITIES:

Admission by card only.

DOROTHY KENYON, *Treasurer.*

A spoof on the Club newsletter issued in 1936, our twenty-fifth anniversary year.

Noted Speakers and Performers 1932–1945

W. H. Auden
Count Basie
Nadia Boulanger
Budapest String Quartet
Padraic Colum
Salvador Dalí
René d'Harnoncourt
Paul Hindemith
Robert M. Hutchins
Lin Yu Tang
Samuel Eliot Morison
Edward R. Murrow
Harold Nicolson
Sergei Prokofiev
Virgil Thomson
Trapp Family Choir

Depression slowly eased but didn't end until President Franklin D. Roosevelt stepped up defense spending in 1940. Cos member Frances Perkins was Roosevelt's Secretary of Labor, the first woman to hold a Cabinet position and a significant shaper of the 1935 Social Security Act.

The Club gave a costume gala on March 15, 1939, "The Cosmopolitan Collection." Members posed as figures in paintings by Vermeer, Sargent, Whistler, Gainsborough, Degas, Goya, and other noted painters. Before the *tableaux vivants* began, there was a Grand March. Josephine Hendrick as George Washington in Trumbull's portrait was enthusiastically applauded, as was Hildreth Meière in Madame X's black velvet less-is-more dress. As always, a good time was had by all. That September, Hitler invaded Poland. Festive parties at the Club would be few and far between for the duration.

Cos members again responded energetically to war in Europe and, two years later, in the Pacific. Pearl Harbor was attacked on a Sunday. The following Wednesday, more than 700 people thronged the Club to hear a talk entitled "Statesmen Look at the Europe of Tomorrow." The speakers were from four German-occupied countries and included Jan Masaryk of Czechoslovakia. Club members enlisted in the WACs, the WAVES, joined medical and other military corps, and nine people on the Club staff were air raid wardens. A War Relief Committee coordinated the Club's war efforts. A workroom was set up on the tenth floor where members produced over 25,000 garments between 1940 and 1945 that were distributed by the Red Cross. They also

The Old Guard as they appeared at the twenty-fifth anniversary party.

Left: Harlequins and clowns after the manner of Picasso, Cézanne, and Severini. (Left to right: Clarinda Lincoln, Mary Cortesi, Elizabeth Hale, Priscilla Pick. Seated: Marcia Hoopes.) Middle: Madame X *by John Singer Sargent as depicted by Hildreth Meière. Right:* George Washington before the Battle of Trenton *by John Trumbull was portrayed by Josephine Hendrick. (All three from "The Cosmopolitan Collection," a program of 1939.)*

knitted socks and sweaters for foreign seamen stranded in New York. The average number of members in that workroom was thirty-five a day, many wearing hats while they worked. In addition, they designed and assembled 1,400 kits for bombed-out or evacuated European and British women, kits that contained small but essential items: a toothbrush, a comb, a pencil, and scissors. The Club-designed kits were the model for thousands produced by other organizations and sent abroad. Even before the war, a radio had been installed in an upstairs sitting room so members could hear broadcasts on foreign policy sponsored by the League of Women Voters; now members listened to hourly bulletins about the war's progress and could also follow it on a war map hanging in the Library. War bonds and stamps were sold weekly at a booth in the Club, and the War Relief Committee raised funds from members to help Europeans in need.

In a radiogram sent to the Club on

Members at work in the War Relief Workroom sometime in the 1940s.

Mannequins dressed in clothes made in the War Relief Workroom.

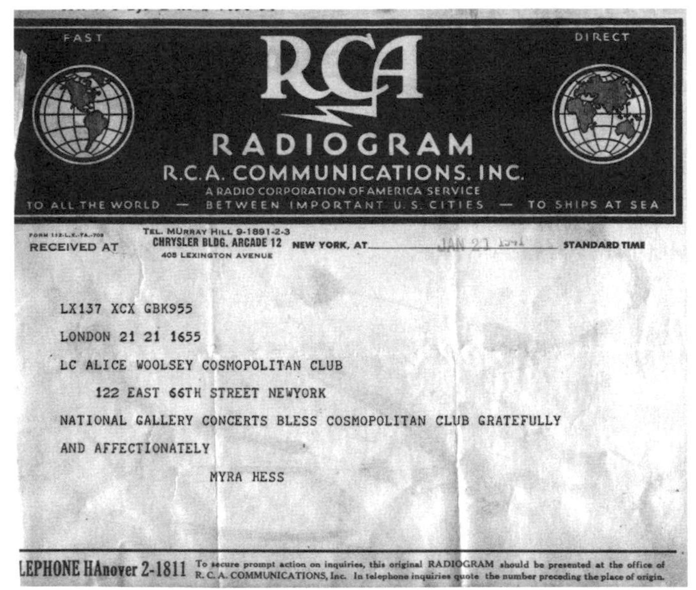

FAST — DIRECT

RCA
RADIOGRAM
R.C.A. COMMUNICATIONS, INC.
A RADIO CORPORATION OF AMERICA SERVICE
TO ALL THE WORLD — BETWEEN IMPORTANT U. S. CITIES — TO SHIPS AT SEA

RECEIVED AT TEL. MURRAY HILL 9-1891-2-3 CHRYSLER BLDG. ARCADE 12 405 LEXINGTON AVENUE NEW YORK, AT JAN 21 1941 STANDARD TIME

LX137 XCX GBK955
LONDON 21 21 1655
LC ALICE WOOLSEY COSMOPOLITAN CLUB
122 EAST 66TH STREET NEWYORK
NATIONAL GALLERY CONCERTS BLESS COSMOPOLITAN CLUB GRATEFULLY
AND AFFECTIONATELY
MYRA HESS

LEPHONE HAnover 2-1811 To secure prompt action on inquiries, this original RADIOGRAM should be presented at the office of R. C. A. COMMUNICATIONS, Inc. In telephone inquiries quote the number preceding the place of origin.

January 21, 1941, Myra Hess thanked her fellow members of the Cos for their support of the free lunchtime concerts at the National Gallery that she organized during the Blitz, concerts that continued until the war ended, lifting spirits in London and, vicariously, on Sixty-sixth Street. In 1948, Dame Myra would come to the Club to thank members in person and to perform at a reception. Henry Steele Commager presented his talk "Britain Looks Ahead"; Eleanor Roosevelt gave her "Impressions of War in the South Pacific." Servicemen enjoyed 79 Monday night dances given in the Cos Ballroom over a four-year period. Classes were held at the Club in first aid, home nursing, and nutrition in times of strict rationing, and a victory garden was planted on the terrace.

The European war ended on May 7, 1945, with Germany's unconditional surrender to the Allies. Three months later, the war in the Pacific ended with a bomb that would forever change the magnitude of destruction that humankind could inflict on itself. Celebrations in the victorious nations were an uneasy tangle of elation, anguish, moral outrage, patriotic pride, remorse, and thanksgiving.

Top: The radiogram sent by a grateful Myra Hess in 1941 to Club President Alice Woolsey. Bottom: Dances for servicemen were held in the Ballroom on alternate Mondays from 1942 to 1945.

The Club's programs have always included international matters. After World War II and the establishment of the United Nations in New York City, the Club's cosmopolitanism became even more pronounced. Cos members Eleanor Roosevelt, Vera Michaeles Dean, Virginia C. Gildersleeve, and Anne O'Hare McCormick participated in the foundation of the UN at a meeting in San Francisco in 1945, forming the Club's ties to the organization, ties cemented when Eleanor Roosevelt was appointed a United States delegate to the UN.

Club members were instrumental in helping foreign women delegates to the UN and the wives and daughters of male delegates adjust to life in New York. The members invited these women, many of whom didn't speak English, to their homes, escorted them on sight-seeing tours, guided them through the complexities of the city and even through a few hospitalizations, and entertained them at the Club. The foreign women reciprocated with cooking demonstrations of their native cuisine and fashion shows of their national dress at the Club and invited Cos members to UN receptions. Strong and lasting friendships were made with the international community. There were monthly Club events called United Nations Sunday Buffet Suppers for members who wanted to meet and talk with international guests. The Club later instituted a new category of membership, Foreign Visitors, now called International Visitors. Today, along with other programs on global issues, the Cos presents monthly talks on international affairs. There are annual International Dinners and Spring Luncheons, highlighted by distinguished speakers, and the Ballroom is always packed to the rafters on those occasions.

In the period immediately following the war, Cos members heard talks on the Marshall Plan, the Nuremberg Trials, the Berlin airlift, recovery in Britain and in Europe, the small but heroic French Resistance movement, Churchill's view of the Iron Curtain's totalitarian consequences in Eastern Europe, Mao Zedong's Communist takeover in China, the new NATO, the role of women in military services, and the Atomic Age. True to Cos form, members also resumed having fun.

The first postwar entertainment was presented at the Annual Meeting in April of 1947, a play called "Strolling in the Park." Helen Hokinson designed backdrop murals for the event, and some of the elaborate costumes were made by members who had sewed in the Club's War Relief Workroom. At the annual spring party, some prominent older members with mirth in mind dressed in baseball uniforms from caps to kneecaps.

The Cos gave a party for the Century Association's hundredth anniversary in 1947; the Century would later give a party for the fiftieth anniversary of the Cos. The two clubs were always closely connected and held many parties for each other over the years. The Cos once gave a "Leap Year Party" for Centurions that was so uproarious it provoked the Club manager, Charles Walton, to ask members "never to repeat such a thing" in the Clubhouse.

Facing page: Eleanor Roosevelt chatting with Adlai Stevenson, Mary Lasker, and Franklin D. Roosevelt Jr. (back to camera) at the Club.

Left: The backdrop for the 1947 production, "Strolling in the Park," was based on this watercolor of Pegasus and the Muses by Helen Hokinson. Right: The celebrated New Yorker *cartoonist at work. The Club has a collection of her original cartoons. Below: Elizabeth Morrow, Florence Blyth, Louisa Jay, and Dorothy Riggs were among the members who donned baseball uniforms for an event of 1947.*

A "chairity" fair held in April 1948 took place throughout the building. There were reportedly hilarious dinners on several floors, after which Club President Mary Ballard Duryee, dressed as sharpshooter Annie Oakley, opened the fair, which featured wandering clowns, village yokels, a weight-guesser, fortune-tellers, an organ grinder, and well-stocked attic trunks for the sale of old clothes and knickknacks. In all, $2,663 was raised for new Ballroom chairs so that Cos women and their husbands and friends would no longer have to writhe in discomfort.

In 1950, the annual spring party at the Club celebrated "The Days When a Woman Had Something to Fight For." Members were asked to dress in costumes that represented American women from the days of the

SPRING 1960

Top left: Club members dressed as one of cartoonist Mary Petty's favorite characters at the "Leap Year Party" for the men of the Century Club, 1964. Top right: Mary Petty's maid, whom she dubbed "Fay," on a New Yorker *cover of March 1941. Below: Drawings Petty made for the Club.*

Poster for "The Days When a Woman Had Something to Fight For," 1950, by Elizabeth Walker Smith. An amateur artist, she produced many posters for Club events from 1950 until the mid 1970s.

Roanoke Colony to the founding of the United Nations, or they could come as their own renowned ancestress, if they had one. There was a preponderance of historic heroines in the pageant: Pocahontas, Western pioneer women, Susan B. Anthony with a cortege of suffragettes, Amelia Bloomer, Harriet Beecher Stowe, Mary Baker Eddy, Emily Dickinson, Emma Lazarus, and Carrie Nation. The pageant concluded in contemporary times with Ruth Cheney Streeter, Jean T. Palmer, Margaret Janeway McClanahan, and Elise E. Sage in their World War II officers' uniforms flanking Virginia Gildersleeve as she read an abridged version of the Preamble to the Charter of the United Nations, which she had helped to write. Despite the up-to-date finale of that pageant, there is a rather wistful edge to it, suggesting as it does the powerful grip of the past. In some ways, the evening may be seen as the last hurrah of the Old Guard at the Cos, women who came of age before World War I when there were important causes to fight for. Women would fight tooth and nail for crucial causes in the next decades, but those were not on the Old Guard's map of the world as they knew and honored it.

Actually, the era of the Old Guard at the Club was long over. It ended in 1932 with the move into the Sixty-sixth Street building when the older women, many of them founders and charter members of the Club, handed over the governance of the organization to younger women. The self-named Old Guard didn't leave their humor and zest for high jinks in the abandoned Fortieth Street quarters. They continued to poke fun at themselves and to participate in revels and pageants, but according to many reports they didn't feel entirely at home in the new Clubhouse, which they found somewhat too formal, not cozy enough, and perhaps a bit bourgeois. Although they enjoyed meeting and talking with younger members, the Old Guard felt their distance from the modern generation at the Cos. Even so, they were inveterate supporters of and socializers at the Club.

Be Chairitable

Have you been dumped
on the Ballroom floor
With shaken bones
and muscles sore?

Has your chair collapsed
while you've been eating
Or sitting quietly
at some meeting?

Then come to the Club
to the Chairity Fair
And spend enough cash
to buy a new chair!

Chairity Fair
Wednesday, April 21st

1948

The decade of the 1950s in America was relatively conventional and conservative, a welcome period of postwar security and stability. In retrospect, it was a ten-year lull before the societal storms ahead. The economy prospered: America liked Ike twice. The so-called Silent Generation, mindful of their schooldays when they ducked and covered for safety, was not inclined to stand up and rock the boat with political and social activism. The Cold War's nuclear threat was real but remote until the Cuban missile crisis in the following decade. Women weren't then aware of their "problem with no name," as Betty Friedan would later describe it. "Countercultural" was not yet in most people's vocabularies.

Things at the Cos were generally in tune with the times. The Club had 1,700 members in 1951 and would have 1,790 by 1959, with one-third of the new members under the age of forty-five. Most of the members were not apathetic or racist or silent women. The Club was officially color-blind in regard to desirable members, as specified in a directive sent by the Board of Governors to the Membership Committee in 1957. Even so, the record shows that a substantial minority of

Lunching in the Members Dining Room about 1950.

Noted Speakers and Performers 1946–1959

Ralph Bunche
Van Cliburn
James B. Conant
Isak Dinesen
Paul Draper
Robert Flaherty
Lincoln Kirstein
David E. Lilienthal
Archbishop Makarios
James Michener
Dorothy Parker
Santha Rama Rau
S. Dillon Ripley
Bertrand Russell
Edith Sitwell
C. P. Snow
Stephen Spender
General Telford Taylor
Arnold J. Toynbee
Eudora Welty

members opposed Marian Anderson's candidacy for membership in 1959. She was nonetheless unanimously elected by the Membership Committee.

Membership in the Club is by sponsorship, not by application. In early days, two personal letters were required in support of a woman's candidacy; today the number is six and the process is lengthier but culminates as it did in the past with what one member called "an ordeal by teacup." When it was suggested in 1967 that Margaret Mead might be spared that ordeal, Mead reportedly said, "Nonsense, nonsense. Tribal rite." She not only participated in the rite, she dressed up for it in a taffeta outfit. One candidate in 1950 bought a new hat from Woolworth's for her tea and was mortally embarrassed to discover afterward that she had left the 69¢ price tag stuck on its front. Her conspicuous thriftiness may have been a plus, as she became a member.

Over the years, the Cos has consistently defined its ideal member as a woman of parts: a person of importance or superior worth. In 1951, the Membership Committee described its "perfect candidate" in a report given at the Annual Meeting as "one [who is] well-rounded; solid without being heavy, strong . . . sturdy and with a certain polish. The flimsy, with a superficial veneer, does not wear well, yet a certain lightness and delicacy is also to be desired. . . . The whole is weighed upon well-balanced scales, regardless of the damage inflicted by time."

In 1953, the summer issue of the *Bulletin* reported the decision of the Finance Committee to start an Investment Fund. For many years, the Club had operated without a margin of safety between income and expenses, and with no provision for major repairs or funds for staff retirement. The committee hoped the Investment Fund would enable the Club to meet economic demands in the future. This hope wasn't fully realized; in 1958, the Club voted to issue a bond for $100,000 to help pay for extensive renovation and redecoration of the buildings on Sixty-sixth and Sixty-fifth Streets. The work was done from May to September of 1958. At the New Members Dinner that November, a skit called "Tea and

Above: Two of twenty-two scenes presented in "New York Stage Revisited," a production of 1953. Left: Mary Schwarz singing "I'm Gonna Wash that Man Right Outa My Hair" from South Pacific. *Right: Emily Belt, center, in the Ziegfeld Chorus.*

Confusion" was performed, a farce inspired by the disturbances caused by the Clubhouse's remodeling.

Even before the Cos faced the expenses of renovation, it had been dealing with soaring labor costs and union demands. Unionization hit all of the city's clubs in 1956, soon after the New York State Labor Relations Board mandated that employees could elect to join unions as the first step to fair and acceptable contracts. The Club's Personnel Policies Committee, chaired by Jean Palmer, the General Secretary of Barnard College and in charge of labor relations there, handled the issue for the Cos, along with Frederica Pisek Barach of the Finance Committee and member Elinore Moorehouse Herrick, a nationally known labor negotiator. On December 19, 1956, the Club signed a contract with the Hotel and Restaurant Employees and Bartenders International Union. In 1958, the Cos started a savings program to finance pension obligations and emergencies. Today, pension funds are in place for union and nonunion Club staff. There have been professional managers since 1933, three of whom worked at the Club for decades, Ernest Garola, Louis Zaberto, and Rita Evans. The Pegasus Fund, supported by members' contributions and service charges added to function bills, provides money for education and training of Club employees and makes holiday gifts to the staff in appreciative recognition of its dedication to the needs of the members throughout the year.

Although the climate of the postwar period wet-blanketed nonconformity, it didn't drench eccentricity in the privacy of the Cos Clubhouse. At a spring party in 1957 the Board of Governors came as ingredients of a seasonal salad, wearing headdresses of wooden bowls

Frederica Barach, Club President, center, signing the contract with the Hotel and Restaurant Employees and Bartenders International Union on December 19, 1956.

After a performance, Pegasus is taken out for a walk.

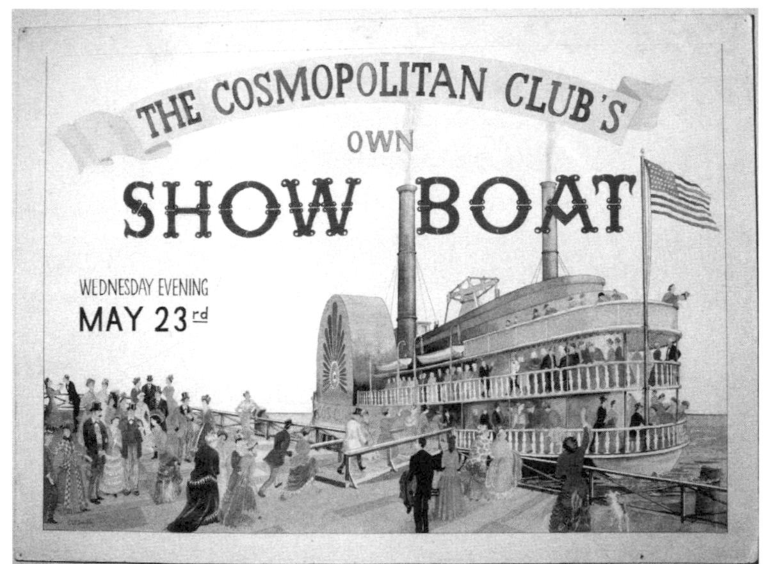

Above left: Poster by Elizabeth Smith for a "Showboat" party that took place on the "nearest thing to a paddle wheeler," a Hudson River dayliner. Right: Members and their guests in costume on board the Peter Stuyvesant, 1956.

filled with radishes or carrots or lettuces or cucumbers, and one wore a black dress with a white sash down the back and a huge cabbage leaf on her head, representing a skunk cabbage.

Members' talks at Tuesday luncheons in the 1950s included Nobel laureate Pearl Buck's "Backgrounds of Formosa" and artist Isabel Bishop's "Today's Painting and Its Traditions." Virginia Pope, fashion editor of the *New York Times*, spoke on Empire and bouffant styles. Poet and humorist Phyllis McGinley presented "The Lighter Side," and, at a tea in the Library, Cornelia Otis Skinner gave a talk on acting.

The 1950s and 1960s were banner years for theatrical presentations at the Club. The stage in the Ballroom had been improved and a new curtain and better lighting had been installed. There were usually two big productions a year performed for three nights to full houses, and several smaller ones created and performed by members at theme parties, New Members Dinners, and other special events. Many of the presentations were produced by Ruth McAneny Loud, the moving spirit of the Drama Committee in those days. She wrote about the members' "hard work, sound achievement, humor and imagination, the chance to try anything—and fun." Members who preferred being backstage designed and painted scenery, made costumes, did props, and worked the lights. A play-reading group met weekly in the Sun Room and provided what Loud recalled as "a wonderful chance for inspired middle-aged ladies to shine as young boys, great lovers, or unlikely females."

The major productions at the Club occasionally featured professionals who were mem-

Golden Anniversary

The fifty years that the Club has been
A valued part of the New York scene
Will pass in an hour on our stage
In tribute to our mounting age
So seize this opportunity
To let our friends and neighbors see
Our gala, golden jubilee!
But first night we members take
To light golden candles on our cake.
The Party should be wonderful
If you'll observe the Golden Rule:
Come in cloth of gold, if you have a piece,
Gold plumes in your hair, or the Golden
Fleece,
As a nugget of gold or a Gold Dust Twin
Or whatever you think you'd be happy in.
What female heart can gold resist?
And you are to be the alchemist.
A heart of gold is not enough.
Please wear a little of the stuff
To celebrate our Fiftieth!

1959

bers. Among the actresses who joined the Cos were Gertrude Lawrence, Mildred Dunnock, Vera Allen, Kitty Carlisle Hart, Patricia Neal, Jessica Tandy, Peggy Wood, Ethel Barrymore Colt, Hope Williams, and Katharine Cornell. In 1952, Noël Coward's *Family Album* was presented with men in the cast, a first for the Club. After that, men performed in many Cos productions and entertainments.

On May 23, 1956, the Cos gave a "Show Boat" party, ferrying 500 members and their guests up the Hudson River under a full moon, all wearing costumes from the period of 1870 to 1900. Partygoers enjoyed dancing, drinking, supper, and a show about old New York, all for $7.50 a ticket. One elderly member, when congratulated in midcruise on being a good sport for coming on the boat trip, asked, "Why the fuss?" If she didn't like the party she could always leave. That she might not be able to walk on water did not appear to faze the adventurous dowager.

The fiftieth anniversary of the Cos was celebrated in 1958–1959 with exhibits of art by members, both professional and amateur, several gala dinners and dances at which members dressed in clothes with golden touches, a professionally tape-recorded production called "Fifty Years in New York" with a cast that included ninety suffragettes and thirteen gentlemen callers. Amey Aldrich's reminiscence about the Cos was published, and many gifts were made to the Library, the Archives, and other parts of the Club. The renovation of the Clubhouse was finished and widely admired, except for the chronically sick air conditioners. Membership was enlarging, and the hum of busyness

A skit at the "Golden Anniversary Party" of 1959.

Above: Yoga class, 1972. Below: "Sing, Sing," by the Melody Quartet, 1970. Left to right: Elizabeth Pilcher, Dorothea Kidder Smith, Olivia Hamilton, Constance Terry.

ON LIVING IN A REVOLUTION. The Public Interests Committee is planning a Fall discussion series for members and guests on coping constructively with drastic social change. The meetings will be held by men and women actively concerned with shifting patterns in key areas of life today.

DO IT YOURSELF. A Fix-It Course is scheduled for four consecutive Wednesday mornings at the Club from 10:00 until noon. Bring your own screwdriver and pliers. Practice material will be provided. Reservations, which are limited, open September 15. Course fee, $20.

The Fix-It Course, under the auspices of the New Leisure Arts Committee, is only one of several other workshops planned for next year. They will include Motor Mechanics (on location at a nearby garage, overalls optional) and Gardening, with the help of experts from the New York Botanical Garden, and further lessons in bridge and cooking courses, which proved so successful this past year.

Advance Notices, Summer *Bulletin*, 1971

in the Clubhouse grew louder daily. It was a truly golden year, and Pegasus was clearly in the ascendant. As a fitting climax to that anniversary, the Century Association gave a party for the Cosmopolitan Club. Eighteen-carat compliments were exchanged and Champagne flowed. Francis T. P. Plimpton, son and husband of Club members, gave a speech in the tradition of his mother, a former Cos Governor who wrote in verse the reports she made at the Annual Meetings. His poem reflected on the sheer beatitude of being a Cos Club consort.

Pegasus may have been on the rise in the 1960s, but the escalating war in Vietnam was a deepening concern. Many other forces reshaped America's political and cultural landscapes over the next two decades, among them the assassinations, violent riots in urban ghettos, the birth control pill, sit-ins and mass marches, consciousness-raising women's groups, youthful rebellion against authority, Woodstock, Stonewall, *Roe v. Wade*, and Watergate. Some of these catalytic events and their impact were topics of discussions at the Club and some were not, but all of them were strongly felt. If 1932 marks the changing of the guard at the Cos, the 1960s and 1970s mark the changing of the Old Guard's granddaughters, women whose everyday lives, roles, sense of purpose, and demands were in the throes of reinvention. In many instances, Cos members didn't need to reinvent themselves; they were already liberated women, independent in thought and in action.

The Cos swayed in the strong winds of the zeitgeist, bending slowly at first, then resolutely adapting to the shifting expectations of its members. "We don't have to be men," said poet Marianne Moore when she spoke at the Club in 1962, "we can be women and do the things men do." It wasn't that simple, but it happened. This became evident at the Club over the next twenty years. The numbers of career women and working mothers in the membership steadily increased, and member-created theatricals and other participatory activities declined. The clothing worn at the Club was different, as were the kinds of classes offered, one of which was a do-it-yourself household repair course. Another, on automobile mechanics, was held at a nearby garage. More events were presented in the evenings when working members could attend them. The sound of rock-and-roll music was heard at Club dances. The Clubhouse bedrooms were opened to so-called proper husbands, one's own, presumably. Club-sponsored trips went farther and farther afield for women who wanted to travel with or without men. There was an expansion of family-oriented events for members with young children or grandchildren. Many other small but palpable innovations were made that would become integral to the milieu and usage of the Club, but it was not until 1981 that members were finally listed in the yearbook by their first or professional names, a major symbolic change reflecting growing independence for women.

The Club's United Nations Committee during these years sponsored workshops on international matters with titles such as "The Impact of Africa on the United Nations," "The Challenge of India," "China, Its History and Its Potential," "The United Nations in Today's World," and "Why Foreign Aid?" Similar workshops were offered on Latin America and the Middle East. In one year alone, 1970, four workshops were announced: "Economic and

Above: Marion Tomkin en route to the Acropolis of Lindos on a Club trip, 1965.

Noted Speakers and Performers 1960–1979

Jacques Barzun
Pierre Boulez
Zbigniew Brzezinski
Jacques d'Amboise
René Dubos
Buckminster Fuller
Brendan Gill
Thomas P. F. Hoving
John Houseman
Robert Joffrey
James Earl Jones
Pauline Kael
George Kennan
John Lindsay
Iris Love
Daniel Patrick Moynihan
George Plimpton
Arthur M. Schlesinger, Jr.
Lewis Thomas

Social Progress," "The Problem of Indochina," "Ecology—Man and His Environment," and "International Cooperation in Outer Space." The study groups usually met in weekly sessions and were addressed by distinguished people in the various fields. There were about fifteen members in each group. One participant, Zelia Peet Ruebhausen, recalled in a taped interview that she had to "do homework and make a report." This was serious education on topical subjects, discontinued when many members began full-time careers.

Still, the Club offered informative talks that didn't require preparatory reading and reports. In that same period, members heard fellow members Barbara Tuchman's "History: Man or System" and retired Wellesley President Margaret Clapp's "Passage to India: One Woman's Experience in an Indian College." Nancy Wilson Ross spoke on young America discovering the East, and Radcliffe President Mary Bunting addressed the waste of opportunities in education. Jessica Daves, former editor-in-chief of *Vogue*, presented "The Great Clothes Rebellion," and writer Francine du Plessix Gray spoke about living in a time of societal revolution. The mother-daughter team of Dorothy Feiner Rodgers and Mary Rodgers Guettel talked about how they "shrank their particular generation gap" and collaborated on a book. Marian Anderson sang, and there was an evening of Shakespeare read by Peggy Wood and Ethel Barrymore Colt. Frequent chamber music concerts took place, as did an exhibit of African

THE COSMOPOLITAN CLUB
122 EAST 66TH STREET
NEW YORK, N.Y. 10021

26 January 1981

TO: All Members
FROM: Hilda Bijur, President
SUBJECT: Grey Book Listing Change

In response to requests during the past few years, we are planning to change the form for the membership roster in the Grey Book. The listings will appear in the 1981-1982 Grey Book as follows:

Smith, Mary Jones (Mrs. John L., Jr.)
Brown, Martha Grace (Miss)
Harris, June Prescott (Mrs.)

If you prefer your listing to remain as it appeared in the 1980-1981 Grey Book please let us know by April 1st.

At the Cleveland Museum of Art, 1971. (Beginning second from left: Margaret Cannon, Gertrude Fay, Penelope Turle, Anne Goodwin, Eloise Spaeth, Ellen Garrison, and an unidentified member.)

Frances Mitchell, Florence Rose, and Janet Dowling in The Chocolate Soldier, *a Broadway hit of 1909, chosen to celebrate the Club's sixtieth anniversary in 1969.*

art from the Brooklyn Museum's collection, many literary events, performances by professional dance companies, visits to members' homes to see their art collections, and several Club-mounted plays.

On the morning of February 12, 1970, there was a fire at the Cos. It started in the kitchen broiler, and the exhaust system carried it up the chimney and onto the roof. Club President Margaret Ogden recalled that she was having breakfast at home when a friend who lived near the Club phoned and said: "Dearie, I think the Cosmopolitan Club is on fire. You'd better get over there right away." Ogden threw on some clothes and ran to Sixty-sixth Street. The firemen had already arrived. They hacked through walls and ceilings to get to the flues, and when they left there was water three inches deep on the kitchen floor. It was pouring through the ceiling below it and cascading into the entrance lobby. No one was hurt, the staff was calm and cooperative, and the ingenuity of the Club's chef and its manager resulted in the Cos not having to cancel a wedding and dinner dance already booked for the Ballroom. During the two weeks of disruption that ensued, members could eat at the nearby Colony Club.

An unusually large deficit was reported at the Club's Annual Meeting in May 1970, only in part due to the expenses incurred by the fire that year. Mounting costs, the decreased use of the Club for dinners and functions, and inflation contributed to the Club's deficit, which mirrored what was happening outside the Clubhouse. The country was heading toward a recession. Unemploy-

The fire at the Club, 1970, as viewed from the terrace of a member who lived on Sixty-seventh Street.

ment rose, the stock market tumbled. New York was only one of the insolvent big cities that lost middle-class population to the suburbs. The Club's shortfall was soon made up by contributions, higher dues, and an ad hoc committee charged with stimulating membership that did its job. The nation's recuperation was slower.

Macaroons

1 pound almond paste
1 pound granulated sugar
6 whites of eggs

Mix almond paste and sugar together well in a beater for 28 minutes slowly.
Then add 1 egg white at a time, one a minute.
Put in pastry bag and squeeze on brown paper.
Each macaroon should be about the size of a silver dollar.
Sprinkle the tops with granulated sugar.
Bake in moderate oven (250-270)

Recipe given by Mr. Garola, Club Manager, to all members, 1973

In 1974, the Abbey Funeral Parlor on the corner of Lexington Avenue and Sixty-sixth Street was sold and the building was demolished. Reliable sources reported that a McDonald's was going to occupy the site. Corpses being carried in and out of a neighboring building in broad daylight may have been objectionable, but a fast-food chain restaurant with its crowds and garbage piling up was entirely out of the question. Club members immediately mounted a protest. They sent letters to Ray Kroc, McDonald's founder and chief stockholder, enlisted the support of Congressman Ed Koch, held street rallies, gathered signatures on petitions, and finally convinced the public relations firm hired by McDonald's that Cos protesters had powerful connections and deep pockets and would not rest until they won their fight. That was that: McDonald's backed down.

Pegasus smiled, quietly.

To revel or not to revel: a burning question first posed at the Club in the early 1960s, a transitional period for women. At a meeting, two schools of Club thought emerged regarding the revel issue, one that "abhorred the idea of dreaming up a costume and coming to an all-female party," and the other with voices raised in the cause of laughter. As the decades of the 1980s and 1990s show, the unabashedly antic diversions of earlier years gave way to sedater entertainment, much of it presented for but not by members. Even so, even subdued, fun for serious women is a bedrock feature of the Cos. Theme parties, humorous programs at New Members Dinners, intellectual exhilaration, and entertaining companionship continued to inspire laughter at the Club.

Shall We About Our Revels?

"Put on your boldest suit of mirth, for we have friends that purpose merriment!"

Come to the revel in honor of Will,
Come in a Farthingale, come in a Frill,
Come in a Doublet, come also in Hose!
Come as a Character everyone knows,
Come as a Play, come as a Sonnet,
Come as a Lad, or a Lass in a Bonnet!
Awards will be made by Good Queen Bess
For wit, ingenuity and beauty of Dress.
If ideas elude just take a look
At a Skinner Collection Costume Book.
You'll find these on the Library shelf,
So step right up and help yourself!
But come to the party and have a good time
As Shakespeare directs, in prose and Rhyme.
Forget you are you, this night in the year,
And join your friends for fun and good cheer!

1949

In response to new pursuits and interests outside of the Clubhouse, financial planning and communication skills workshops were offered in 1983, along with writing groups, foreign language classes, an acting workshop, yoga, and tap dancing. The format of the Annual Meeting was changed to make it shorter and more appealing. The House Rules still specified jackets and ties for men in the Clubhouse and banned blue jeans and shorts from the premises. The service by the staff was as proper and polite as ever. Gracious civility continued to be the standard of behavior at the Club. Despite the overlay of residual correctitude, the fundamental tone of the Cos was increasingly casual, and it became an easier gathering place for women whose lives were a difficult juggling act of personal, professional, and familial responsibilities and activities.

The Club was seventy-five years old in 1984. Several celebrations were planned for the year, a questionnaire was sent to the membership to survey their feelings about and suggestions for the Club, and a Long Range Planning Committee was formed. That committee met monthly during 1984 and 1985, and its report to the Board of Governors focused on three

Facing page: Pegasus played by Louisa Harris takes a bow at a New Members Dinner.

"The Ballad of the Cosmopolitan Club" presented in 1941 in celebration of the thirtieth anniversary of the Club's incorporation.

contemporary Club concerns: space and its use, computerization, and New York City's anti-bias bill, enacted in 1965. Some of the committee's recommendations were soon followed, such as the closing of the hairdressing salon and, more gradually, the computerization of the offices and records.

Fashion show of 1982 celebrating the fiftieth year in the present Clubhouse. Left: Isabel Van Dine in member Elizabeth Rinehart's maternity dress. Right: Linda Storrow in designer Vera Maxwell's 1941 Rosie the Riveter jumpsuit.

The Cos enrolled 98 new members that anniversary year, bringing the number to an effective maximum of 1,300 Resident Members, 700 Nonresident Members, 22 Foreign Visitors, now called International Visitors, and 26 Associate Members, a category replaced by Younger Members. The finances of the Club were in good shape despite rising costs of staff labor, building repairs, supplies, and, again, a declining stock market. Dues for Resident Members were $775 and the initiation fee was $1,200. Younger members paid less. Cos dues were always kept as moderate as possible to accommodate women working part-time or for low salaries. Making ends meet at the Club was difficult but doable, and was done.

On January 30, 1984, a cocktail party kicked off the celebratory year. In April, a musical skit, "On Others' Toes: An Off, Off, Oh So Off Broadway Production," was presented and performed by Cos singers and tap dancers. Part of that evening's program was a parade of historically typical Club members from Governess to Grande Dame to Flapper to Flower Child to Today's Woman. Distinguished speakers that year included members Donna Shalala, Rumer Godden, Trude Wenzel Lash, Eleanor Jackson Piel, and Melanie Kahane. The November 14 final jubilee event was a seventeenth-century Elizabethan frolic performed by the Capricorn Theatre Company with several Cos members in the cast. Music, colorful pageantry, revelry, a gala dinner, and dancing all evoked the amusing festivities of the Club's past.

Yo-Yo Ma and Emmanuel Ax performed at a Club concert, 1983.

HAIRDRESSING DEPARTMENT PRICES	
Haircut	$1.00
Scalp Treatment	$2.00
Wella Kolestrol Treatment with Shampoo	$5.00
Shampoo—Plain	$1.25
Shampoo—Cream	$1.75
Shampoo—Milk	$1.75
Shampoo—Egg	$1.75
Hair—Hand Dried	$ .75
Rinses	$ .50
Finger Wave	$2.00
Marcel Wave	$1.50
Manicure	$1.25
Manicure—Oil	$1.75
Facial—Clean-up	$2.00
Facial—with Back Treatment	$5.00
Eye Brow Arch	$ .75
Wax Treatments	$1.50
Permanent	$15.00
Permanent—Cold	$20.00

1940s

In 1987, an entirely unamusing though anticipated issue arose at the Club: gender discrimination. Three men filed complaints of bias against two Manhattan women's clubs, the Cos and the Colony, with the New York State Division of Human Rights. They claimed they had been refused membership in the clubs, an infringement of their constitutional and statutory rights. Needless to say, the media circus came to town and parked itself in front of the Cos and the Colony. The complaint sprang from growing pressure on the city's social clubs for compliance with Local Law 63, passed in 1965, that prohibited discrimination based on race, religion, or sex in places of public resort or amusement. That law was amended in 1984 to exempt only those clubs that were distinctly private in nature and did not serve to further trade or business. The Governors of the Cos and the Colony, realizing that they might be subject to challenges regarding their membership, had met together to discuss the situation and how to handle it; neither club expressed any enthusiasm for admitting men. The Cos responded by appointing an ad hoc Legal Committee that wrote a statement about the Club's status and practices. This was sent to the New York City Human Rights Commission along with copies of the Club Charter, By-laws, House Rules, and a sworn affidavit that the Club was a private social club in type and in the use of its facilities. The packet of documents evidently convinced the Commission that the Cos was not subject to the anti-bias statute and that the complaint was invalid.

Menu cover for an international dinner, 1989.

Wall Street had its worst day ever on October 19, 1987. Once again, the American economic picture was a study in grim. In the unshakable belief that laughter in the dark is helpful, the Cos gave a "Tax Break Dance" in 1987 with a special dinner menu that featured Currency of Cucumber Soup, Golden Fleece Filet Mignon, a Strawberry Rebate Surprise with Fortune Five Hundred Cookies, U.S. Mints, and Deregulated Coffee. Another occasion for levity that year was a "Famous Lovers Dance," at which costumed members appeared as Adam and Eve, Eliza Doolittle and Professor Henry Higgins, Count and Countess Dracula, Hester Prynne and Reverend Arthur Dimmesdale, and Lieutenant Pinkerton and Cio-Cio San, also known as Madame Butterfly.

> In eighteen hundred and fifty-five
> Hardly a man is now alive—
> Anyway none who matter—
> Who dares deny that that was when
> We women set out to conquer the men
> With reason instead of chatter.
> We struggled to pierce the great unknown.
> We fought for a name to call our own
> Like Dorothy Dix or Lucy Stone,—
> Particularly the latter.
> We mobilized and hypnotized our talent,
> To see the struggle through,
> We fought the fight so gallantly
> There's nothing left to do.
>
> *Verse by Nancy Hamilton from "The Days When a Woman Had Something to Fight For," 1950*

Members who spoke at Tuesday lunches in the 1980s included Alice Stone Ilchman on women's equity in the workforce, Barbara Scott Preiskel on corporate social responsibility, Margaret Osmer McQuade about television news, Christine von Wedemeyer Beshar on wills and taxes, Nannerl Overholser Keohane on women and authority. Katherine Meyer Graham talked about press issues, Colette Mahoney on religious women as professionals and executives, Joan Wiener Konner about what was missing in broadcast journalism, Judge Kathryn Austin McDonald on the Family Court, and Elaine Hiesay Pagels on the politics of sexuality, freedom, and human nature in the book of Genesis. Jill Ker Conway and Carolyn Gold Heilbrun talked about their work. Members enjoyed visits to museums, private collections, and artists' studios, theater and opera outings, and concerts in the Clubhouse. The Club presented a symposium on feminism that included panelists Gloria Steinem and Elizabeth Janeway. There were trips abroad and throughout the city, including a tour of the devastation in the South Bronx, a visit to the White House, and a

Two members of the Cos Club Tappers, Edna Gurewitsch and Josephine Raymond, at a Club gala, 1991.

Noted Speakers and Performers 1980–1999

R. W. Apple, Jr.
Louis Auchincloss
Emmanuel Ax
McGeorge Bundy
Robert A. Caro
Kenneth B. Clark
Alistair Cooke
Philippe de Montebello
Robert Fitzgerald
Carlos Fuentes
Shirley Hazzard
Skitch Henderson
John Hollander
P. D. James
Robert Kennedy, Jr.
Paul LeClerc
Glen D. Lowry
Yo-Yo Ma
Ismael Merchant
Nigel Nicolson
Charlie Rose
Harrison E. Salisbury
Marian Seldes
Brian Urquhart

At a 1990 dinner, members were asked to dress in vintage clothing. Poster by Meredith Hamilton.

picnic at Val-Kill, the home of the Club's beloved member Eleanor Roosevelt. All in all, it was a high-protein feast for thought.

Since 1980, the Associate Members Committee had been planning events that would engage their younger age group, and two were given in 1994. In 1988 and again in 1994, members heard two series of talks on the subject of successful healthy aging, of increasing concern as the elderly population in the Club and in the world grows. There was something of interest for members of every age, classes in French, Spanish, and Italian, life drawing, bridge and chess, book groups, exercise workouts, yoga and tap dancing, seminars on current developments in the stock and bond markets, computer workshops, programs on political affairs and environmental issues, concerts and talks, and more. Today, when age is said to be only a

number, not a condition, the lines that used to divide young from old are blurred and stretchy. This is apparent at the Club's multigenerational gatherings at events and meals and parties. The intermingling of ages and of life experiences is often spoken of as a feature that attracts people to the Cos. The upper limit for admission as a younger member was formerly thirty-five. Now, it is fifty. Once upon a time, fifty was over the hill.

At the Annual Meeting in 1994, the Club reported its financial soundness. There were 86 new members who worked in many fields, including health care, finance, law, television production, and music. That year, the Club embarked on a ten-year strategic plan that would enable it to commit funds for capital improvements of its buildings. Members' talks included Judith Burns Jones's "Children in Poverty: Combating America's Real Deficit" and Virgilia Heinsath Pancoast's "Fakes in Art: Exposing the Art of Deception." Ambassador Louise Fréchette presented "The U.N. Today: A Time of Hope, A Time of Challenge." These are just three of the Club's varied programs in a single year. There were also the traditional parties, dances, and entertainments, some of them self-spoofing, another tradition at the Club.

At the New Members Dinner in 1996, a skit called "A Feminist's Fantasy" was performed to music from *H.M.S. Pinafore* with a cast that included a chorus and tap dancers. The plot revolved around a young man related to generations of Cos members who wanted to join the Club. He dressed as a woman, went to the requisite tea, was admitted as a member, but then confessed to his actual gender, whereupon he was promptly rejected and advised to marry a Cos woman so he could use the Club.

The restoration of the Ballroom and its adjacent areas was done in 1998–1999 when Janet Rodes Hester was Club President, and included modernization of the mechanical systems. The leaky skylights in the Ballroom alcoves were replaced, and they and the loggia leading to the Sixty-fifth Street building were again bright and useful spaces. In an oral history interview, Hester told an amusing story about the Ballroom's discarded cloth hangings. A member asked for the fabric, which was gold-colored with a Chinese motif. She took it home, ran

Above: A poster by Joan Middleton for a 1994 party, "Le Carnaval."

The Loggia, recently restored, as it appeared in 1933.

it through her washing machine, and used it to cover two sofas, demonstrating yet again the proverbial wisdom of waste not, want not.

Noted Speakers and Performers 2000–2008

Joan Acocella
Ayaan Hirsi Ali
William G. Bowen
Billy Collins
Gail Collins
Judy Collins
Thelma Golden
Linda Greenhouse
John Kerry & Teresa Heinz Kerry
William H. Luers
Jacques Pépin
James Stewart Polshek
Christine C. Quinn
Andy Rooney
Robert Rosenblum
Queen Silvia of Sweden
Anne-Marie Slaughter
Pauline Trigère
Mike Wallace
John Wilmerding
James D. Wolfensohn

The millennium arrived, and Pegasus flew into it briskly. At Tuesday lunches in 2000, members heard "Reflections for the Millennium," a talk by Evelyn Hausner Lauder. Hanna Holborn Gray presented "Millennial Thoughts on Higher Education," and Agnes Gund spoke about building a museum for the twenty-first century. The Arts and Interests Committee increased the number of spoken-word events, and raised the honorariums for speakers in an effort to attract interesting and important nonmember speakers, an effort that was only mildly successful until the Club amended its bylaws in 2005 and allowed the sale of lecturers' and musicians' recently published books or recordings after they finished their talks and performances. This change would bring to the Club such distinguished speakers as Supreme Court Justice Stephen G. Breyer, former FBI Director Louis Freeh, Governor Christine Todd Whitman, President of the Carnegie Corporation Vartan Gregorian, and Nobel laureates Sir Paul Nurse and Professor Joseph Stiglitz.

The events of September 11, 2001, and their continuing aftermath gave rise to new topics for talks at the Cos. Members wanted, needed, and got hard information from diplomats, historians, politicians, Middle East scholars, journalists, military experts who spoke on terrorism, the backlash against America, the looting of the Baghdad Museum, and the Iraqi judicial system. In addition, talks on the political and economic situations in North Korea, China, and India, and other global concerns helped members frame different and larger views of the changing world they live in. The roster of speakers was impressive, prompting a member to remark that the listings she saw in the Cos

Andi Emerson, Supreme Court Justice Stephen Breyer, and Susan Montgomery, 2005.

1.

THE COSMOPOLITAN CLUB
122 EAST 66th STREET
NEW YORK, N.Y. 10021

Dear House committee,

Just a word to say how grateful I am to you and the staff for making my stay at the "Cos."

2.

Bulletin were as stimulating as those she read in the *New Yorker.*

In line with the latest communication technology, the *Bulletin* is now online. The Cos Web site was launched in April 2004. Members can visit the Web site to read the *Bulletin,* make event reservations, and access the Library's digitized catalog.

Also in keeping with up-to-dateness, the Sixty-fifth Street building was extensively renovated in 2005. The comptroller's office was moved back to Sixty-sixth Street and the space was converted to a studio for exercise and dance classes. In 2006, work was done inside and on the exterior of the Sixty-sixth Street building, the public and guest rooms were refreshed, and a new kitchen was installed.

The Club's diverse programs were always well attended, but it is the Member Luncheons that are a core activity of the Cos. To accommodate working members, the talks begin and end strictly on schedule, and lecture-only participants are welcomed. Personal reminiscences continue to be of particular interest, and engaging talks were given by Edna Perkel Gurewitsch, Ruth W. Friendly, Edith Kunhardt Davis, Honor Moore, Cecily Cannon Selby, Reeve Lindbergh, Louise Meière Dunn, Laura Huizinga Conley, the presidents of

Above: An illustrated thank-you letter from member Renée Graubart to the House Committee after a stay at the Club.

The cast of "The Missing Muse," performed at the New Members Dinner of 2000. Standing left to right: Elizabeth Ecker, Dorothy Compagno, Kayo Parker, Denise Clayton, Susan Montgomery, Karen Glanternik, Marjorie Shapiro, Norma Flender, Mary Libby, Janet Desforges. Sitting: Judy Inglis, Janet Nelson, Eve Wolf, Victoria Larson. Reclining: Kitty Benton.

Wellesley, Vassar, Smith, and Barnard, and many other members.

A second activity central to the Cos are the committee meetings. When Club manager Rita Evans was interviewed in 2006 for the oral history archives, she said: "The success of the Cos Club [is] the strength of its committees. I remember sitting down and counting; twenty-two percent of our membership is on a committee." This is a sizable but unsurprising percentage; members were always eager to give their time and expertise to the Club. Although many of today's members are professional women who have fewer, if any, hours to volunteer for committee work, the Club's thirty-two committees and subcommittees are as vigorous as ever. They have an essential role in the functioning of the Club and, as a valuable fringe benefit, provide members with an opportunity to meet and make new friends.

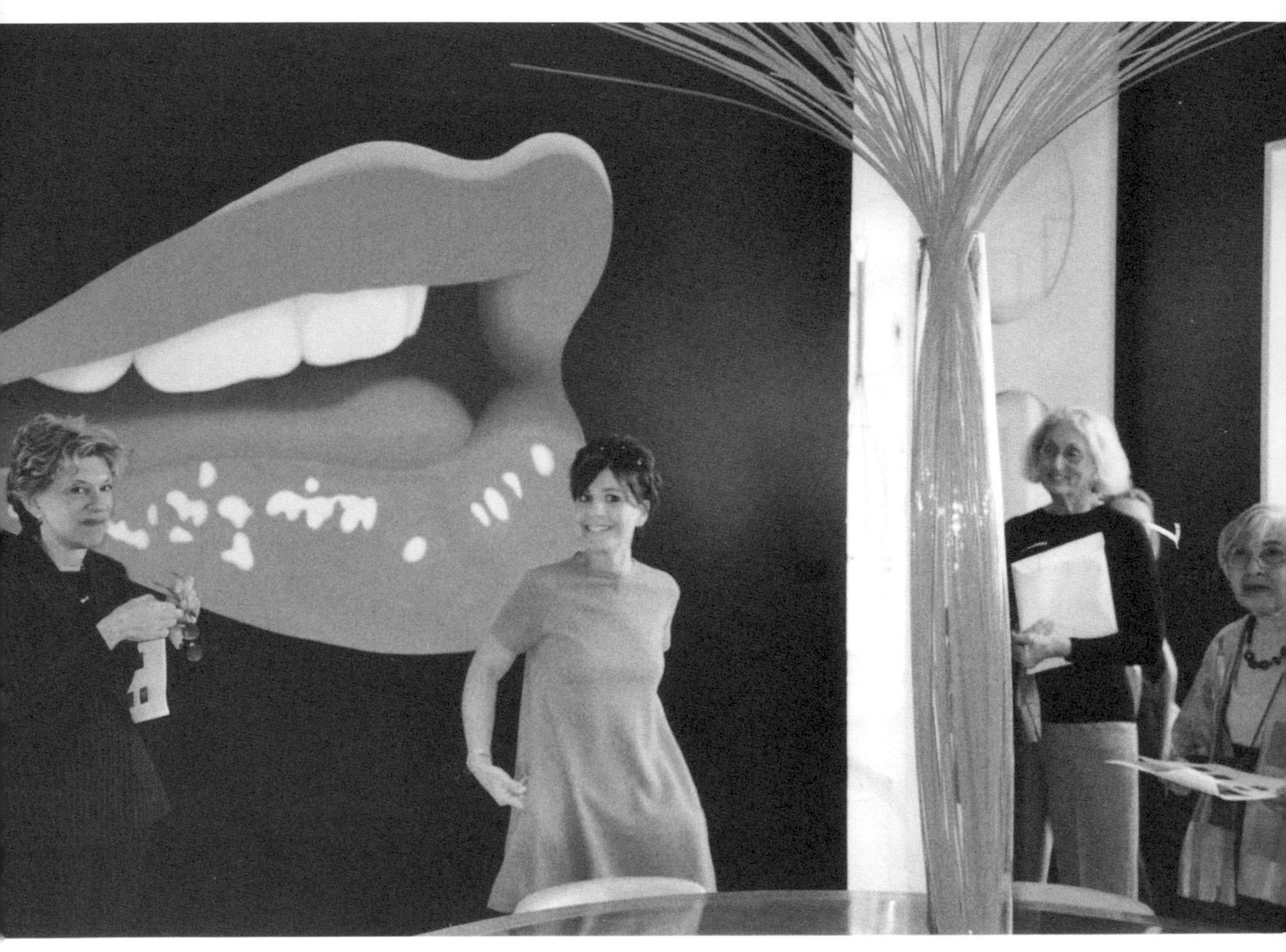

A 2006 visit to the Pop Art collection of Lisa Perry, who stands in front of Mouth *by Tom Wesselman. To her right: Ina Schnell, Ruth Turner.*

Arts and Interests Committee meeting, October 2005. On left: Evelyn Halpert, Jeanne Dickinson, Jocelyn Chait, Chair Cynthia Schaffner, Jessie Palmer, Christine Miller Martin, Charlotte Armstrong, Barbara Kummel, Ellen Marcus. On right: Andi Emerson, Beth Gleick.

The following was reported at the Annual Meeting in May 2008. The Club had 2,019 members, of whom 22 were Life Members, 1,537 were Resident Members, and 460 were Nonresident Members, 35 of them living abroad. Nine membership teas were given in 2007–2008, and the Club welcomed 88 new members ranging in age from their early thirties to their seventies, with the average age of fifty-eight. Many of the new members were professionals in such fields as education, health care, media, finance, the arts, real estate, and philanthropy. The Fall Activities Guest Program, a two-year trial to begin in the fall of 2008, was announced. Guests accepted into the program, which runs for a period of three months, will get to know Club members and the events and social activities at the Cos. The Arts and Interests Committee and its sixteen subcommittees responsible for the wide variety of programs, publications, classes, receptions, and many other Club functions, presented 195 events at the Club between September and July. Workshops in financial planning and flower arranging were offered to members. The Library Committee completed the digitization of the card catalog. In honor of the upcoming centennial of the Cos, the library subscription

Dance Committee of the "Masquerade Ball," 2004. Left to right: Julia Horner, Meredith Rigg, Henrietta Robinson, Paula Timmerman, Penny Davis, Catherine Brawer, Phyllis Bartlett, Holly Hunt.

fee was permanently dropped, allowing members to take out books from the Club's collections without additional expense. Approximately a hundred members attended each of the Member Luncheons held every Tuesday in January, February, and March of 2008. There were 1,193 registrations for classes given at the Club, and a new beginners' ballet class for children was offered. A large majority of members used the Cos Web site to make event reservations. The Club was affiliated with thirty-six clubs on three continents, all of them offering reciprocal privileges to Cos members. Despite rising costs of labor, food, and insurance, the Club's revenues exceeded the expenses of its operating budget. The staffing of the Club was reorganized, and five managerial positions were created and filled. The Club had 59 versatile and talented

Cos Club Summer Lunches presently take place on Long Island, Martha's Vineyard, and Nantucket, and in Northwest Connecticut. Pictured at the Martha's Vineyard Lunch of 2006 are, left to right in back row: Constance Ellis, Margery Oakes, Linda Schapiro, Gayle Lee, Wendy Jeffers, Gail Rodney, Chantal Hodges, Robin Rivera, Suzanne O'Connor, Gail Goltra, Frances Dennison, Carolyn Moses. Front row: Charlotte Armstrong, Miriam Siffert, Elizabeth Beim. Seated: Rona Kiley, Patricia Neal.

full-time and 2 part-time employees. The numbers in these reports confirmed the ongoing appeal and robust condition of the Cos.

Club Presidents speak at the Annual Meeting, and two of these talks resonate in today's world. Both touch on the role of the Cos in troubled times.

In 1948, Mary Ballard Duryee looked for "a directive in confusion. . . . This is a time to take stock of ourselves and shed, wherever we can, the superficial and showy accessories that only clutter up our lives. In an over-mechanized civilization, one thing is increasingly certain: that we must be more than 'mothers of invention' if we are going to build a habitable world. A fresh value then is apparent in companionship, in the creative arts, in the ways of gracious living and gentle manners, in the capacity of having fun together. . . . The climate

Facing page: At the Annual Meeting, 2008.

here at the Club nurtures those things in the city that keep human beings human, hearts warm instead of cold—and this has always been and is today the best personal defense against aggression and hate."

These words were echoed and reinforced by Rebecca Jackson Sargent in 1989, when she said: "Let us be sure that prospective members understand the nature of our Club and the qualities it cherishes. We are not a professional club, although we are most fortunate in our professional members. . . . [We are] a social club for the use and benefit of women engaged in the liberal arts or professions. This implies shared interests and mutual respect and consideration. Ours is a club which is an end in itself and not a means to an end. In our current environment where so many members are addressing unsolvable issues, the Cosmopolitan Club represents a veritable oasis, a resource of serenity and refreshment from which we derive new energy and strength of purpose."

The troubles changed in our times, the Cos remains a warm and invigorating oasis in the city, a space imbued with a durable sense of community, so precious in our unstable world. The original goals of spirited friendliness and intellectual nourishment are as cohesive as ever. The Club's outstanding programs attract large audiences, despite competition from hundreds of events available every day and evening in New York City. Cos presentations cover the arts, politics, education, women's issues, history, finance, sciences, and philanthropy. These are the very same subjects that excited and inspired the Club's founding members, but today's members have different ideas and feelings about them. Women came into their own during the century of the Cosmopolitan Club's existence. There is no end to what is still ahead for women, no ending to our Club's still-evolving life story.

The Cos in the Life of Its Members

Drawings by Joan Middleton

122

Founders and Early Members

What first led me into our Archives was an aunt's claim that my grandmother Emily V. Sloan Hammond had been a Club founder. This was plausible. Granny was a demon organizer, a founder of the Parents League, whose presidency she hung on to for seventeen years. I discovered at the Cos Club, however, that she had been a charter member, nothing more. My research into our early history aroused my curiosity about our founders and early Club members. Here is some of what I found.

Seven members signed our papers of incorporation on March 16, 1911. The first three listed are Edith Carpenter Macy (1870–1925), Ethel Phelps Stokes Hoyt (1877–1952), and Adele Herter (ca. 1869–1946). All three came from or were allied to leading families of the city. Edith Macy and her husband, V. Everit, a Quaker heir to an oil fortune, were benefactors of Teachers College and many other institutions. They sat on countless committees and boards both here in the city and in Westchester County. At her death in 1925 she was chair of the National Board of the Girl Scouts. She appears to have played a pivotal role in founding our Club.

Ethel Hoyt was the eighth of the ten children of the hugely successful merchant banker Anson Phelps Stokes. The youngest of the Club's incorporators, she was the first treasurer and, later, chair of the Finance Committee. Her major interest became the role of religion in maintaining good health, a subject on which she lectured widely and wrote a book.

Adele Herter was of a different stripe. A professional portrait painter, she had met her husband, Albert, son of one of the cofounders of Herter Brothers, the noted decorating firm, while they were art students in Paris. Her commissioned portraits included ones of Edith Macy and Abby Rockefeller. As well as being painters, both Herters had a great talent for decoration, a skill they used to embellish their estate, The Creeks, in East Hampton, and their large house, El Mirasol, in Santa Barbara.

Of our four other incorporators, Josephine Pomeroy Hendrick (1863–1962), Helen Gilman Brown (1867–1942), Abby Aldrich Rockefeller (1874–1948), and Mary Ashley Hewitt (1865–1945), Mrs. Hendrick did most to shape the Club. Chairman of entertainment before incorporation, later chair of Arts and Interests and the subcommittee on Literature and Drama, she can be credited for the outstanding programming and diverting entertainments such as the Revels. When ninety-three, Mrs. Hendrick was persuaded to write of her long and interesting life for the *New Yorker.*

Helen Gilman Brown, wife of a religion professor, had authored a biography of an early head of Phillips Academy in Andover before becoming Club President in 1911. After her term ended, Mrs. Brown, clearly a first-rate administrator, became national president of the Woman's Land Army, finance chair of the YWCA, and president of the National Society of Colonial Dames.

Mrs. Hewitt and Mrs. Rockefeller both had fathers who were prominent politicians. Mary Ashley Hewitt lived in Montana as a child when her father was named governor of that territory. She married the son of a New York mayor who was also a grandson of Peter Cooper. She chaired the New York Association for the Blind and helped organize the Public Education Association. Her play *The Parasitic Woman* was performed at the Club in 1915. Abby Aldrich Rockefeller's role in founding MoMA in 1929 is too well known to expand on here.

The founders, then, were take-charge women, eager to participate in the wider world and to seize the opportunities being opened up for women by the suffrage movement and World War I.

The early governors were drawn from a more diverse group. They included the educators Maria Bowen Chapin and Elizabeth Carse; Leta Brace Croswell, wife of the head of the Brearley School; the actress Harriet Otis Dellenbaugh; and the acclaimed writer of Southern tales Ruth McEnery Stuart. Born in 1850 in Louisiana, she took up the pen to earn a living when, mother to one and stepmother to eleven, she was widowed in 1883.

Two Bryn Mawr graduates, Caroline McCormick Slade (1874–1951) and Helen Thomas Flexner (1871–1951), played important roles. Mrs. Flexner came to New York when her husband, a pathologist, was appointed first director of the Rockefeller Institute. In 1940 she wrote of her youth in A *Quaker Childhood: 1871–1881.* Mrs. Slade was a prominent suffragette as were two other Club members, Katherine Ludington, a painter and head of the Connecticut Woman Suffrage Association, and Narcissa Cox Vanderlip, who chaired the New York State League of Women Voters from 1919 to 1923.

The women of the Cosmopolitan Club deserve a whole book. This is but a tiny sampling.

Sophia Duckworth Schachter

The Cosmopolitan Club and the World of Education

When I joined the Cosmopolitan Club in 1975, shortly after becoming Head of the Brearley School, I learned that the Club can trace its origin to the teaching profession. At a time when the line between governesses and teachers of young children was not sharply drawn, the Club began as a place where governesses could gather on weekends and invite guests to tea. For its first two years, it was housed at the Froebel League on East Sixtieth Street, a training college for kindergarten teachers named for Friedrich Froebel, the nineteenth-century German educator who invented the word *kindergarten*.

An early draft for the new club's constitution indicated that it was intended to serve "any self-supporting gentlewoman acting in an educational capacity in the school or home," and while the admissions criteria, after the Club moved to new quarters on East Thirty-third Street, soon expanded to include "women of either professional attainment or definite interest in the arts and professions," from the start the Club counted teachers among its leading members. Its first president was a school principal, Elizabeth Carse (of the Charlton School, which has since disappeared). In 1913, when the Club moved to Fortieth Street, the opening event in its new location, cosponsored by the president of the New York City Board of Education, was a reception for Dr. Maria Montessori. Maria Bowen Chapin, founder of the Chapin School, was on the Club's first Board of Governors, and in 1914 Clara Spence, founder of the Spence School, became a member, as did Virginia C. Gildersleeve, a Brearley alumna and dean of Barnard College.

Over the years, teachers, professors, school principals, college and university presidents, educational activists, and trustees of educational institutions across the country have played major roles in the Club, sponsoring a rich array of programs. Women college presidents abound among the Club's members. Speakers have included presidents of all the leading women's colleges and women presidents of coed colleges and universities. Talks on education figured prominently in the earliest Member Luncheons. In 1920, Mrs. Dwight Morrow, then president of the Smith College Alumnae Association, spoke on "College Women"; in 1924, Virginia Gildersleeve spoke on "International Friendship Through University Women"; in 1926, Ada Louise Comstock, president of Radcliffe, spoke on "International Scholarship"; and in 1928, Millicent Carey McIntosh, then acting dean of Bryn

Mawr College but soon to return as head of Brearley and later as president of Barnard College, spoke on "Random Reflections of a School Mistress."

True to its origins, the Club has served generations of school heads and teachers in preschool programs and primary and secondary schools as well as the parents whose children attend them. In 1913, Cos Club members were instrumental in creating the Parents League of New York, and one of the first things I learned when I became head of Brearley was that the Guild of Independent Schools, an organization of heads of independent schools throughout the greater New York area, holds its regular meetings at the Cos Club, discussing issues of concern in education. Many of my colleagues from the Guild are Cos Club members, as are teachers from their schools, and a recent initiative of the Library Committee, inviting English teachers from New York schools to lead afternoon and evening book discussions, is just one example of the ways in which the Club benefits from the presence of outstanding teachers in our midst.

The Club's educational outreach, of course, is not limited to private schools, colleges, and universities. The subject of a 1927 Member Luncheon was "The Citizen and the Public School," and later speakers have addressed such topics as "The Rocky Road to Better Schools," "The State University: Problems and Prognostications," "The World as an Environmental Classroom," "The Harlem School of the Arts," "John Dewey and American Education: Perspectives on the Present," "Park and 119th Street: A Storefront School and Its Community," and "Parent Power: Can It Change the Public Schools?" Clearly, education in all its aspects has been a matter of keen and abiding interest to the Cos Club throughout its first hundred years.

EVELYN J. HALPERT

Five Decades

The Cosmopolitan Club occupied an important place in my imagination long before I ever set foot in it. I'd arrived in the United States from Australia in 1960 to take a doctorate in American History at Harvard. My dissertation was a study of the first generation of American women to undertake graduate education, among them the great Progressive era reformers Jane Addams, Lillian D. Wald, Florence Kelley, and Julia Lathrop, women who particularly attracted me.

Wald, a Club member, was a quintessential New Yorker, utterly involved, as founder and leader of the Henry Street Settlement, in the politics of the city and the nation. Kelley moved to New York to found the National Consumers' League and to help launch the International Ladies' Garment Workers' Union, working to end sweatshops. Addams and Lathrop, another Club member, crisscrossed the country from their respective bases at Hull-House in Chicago and the Federal Children's Bureau in Washington, working to end sweat-

shops. Every trip seemed to end up in New York at the Cosmopolitan Club. Jane Addams, a formidable correspondent, made me feel as though I had been at the luncheon held in her honor on East Thirty-third Street and had stayed in the room she described to friends after a stay at the Fortieth Street Clubhouse. From the way her usually measured tone gave way to superlatives I could tell how impressed she was by the architecture and decoration on what was perhaps her only visit to East Sixty-sixth Street.

Reading through these women's papers, I came to know the Club's letterhead well. Before the days of casual use of the telephone a member's arrival would be marked by an explosion of letters from the Club to organize schedules, arrange meetings, invite friends to lunch and dinner.

My research on the history of American women introduced me to the importance of women's clubs in the post–Civil War era as providers of social space where women could meet without any question of impropriety. Before their arrival a woman couldn't be seen in a restaurant or at a concert without a male escort, so early clubs were important in providing women with independence to move around a city. I was delighted to learn about the early history of the Cosmopolitan Club, which explained its focus on intellectual and professional women.

When I became president of Smith College in 1975 I gladly accepted an invitation to become a member. Because I was in New York frequently for days packed with meetings, I often arranged to dine alone at the Club to assimilate the events of the day and reflect on what I'd learned about fund-raising. Sometimes as I settled into my own reflections over good food and drink I noticed other women dining alone whose dress and manner made me certain that they must be retired faculty from Barnard or Hunter. They walked briskly into the dining room, ordered a double martini and a bowl of soup, and proceeded to enjoy both before, with total sangfroid, producing a ham sandwich from a brown paper bag while ordering coffee.

After I discovered the beautiful and spacious double rooms available to couples, the Club became a place of pleasure and relaxation. Life in the Smith College president's house was always enjoyable but crowded with official guests and college functions. So John Conway and I would escape to East Sixty-sixth Street, sink into the quiet and luxury of one of those double rooms, and set about enjoying New York, the Metropolitan Opera, and lazy Sunday mornings.

Although there are many places for me to stay in Manhattan these days, I still find the Club the most comfortable of them all, rivaling any of the luxury hotels that keep appearing in the city. I love to arrive in my room, fling open the window overlooking the garden, gaze out at the skyline, and know that I am *home*. As I drop off to sleep I amuse myself by wondering what budding Jane Addams or Willa Cather or Ellen Glasgow may be nodding off next door. In the daytime, I savor spending time in the public rooms and relish observing my fellow club members. They could be, it seems to me, from no place else in the world but New York. Their faces, their energy, their dress, their voices—all convey a distinctive culture.

We began in a stable, moved to a garage, and then created our own landmark in our first century, and we can be sure that our second will see equally profound and creative transformations, drawing, as always, on the capacity of our membership and leaders to get things right.

Jill Ker Conway

Our Members in the Professions

The Cosmopolitan Club started life, a century ago, as something different and remains so to this day. Our founders, themselves women of intellect and stature, responded to the felt need of governesses in their employ, women of intelligence and many talents and interests, for intellectual stimulation and companionship on their days off in a city of strangers.

In the early years, as the Club's membership grew and diversified, the professions became more varied. Surprisingly, we had a number of doctors, and other professions were well represented: the arts, architecture, theater, literature, and journalism. The early members also included academics and entrepreneurs, some with their own businesses.

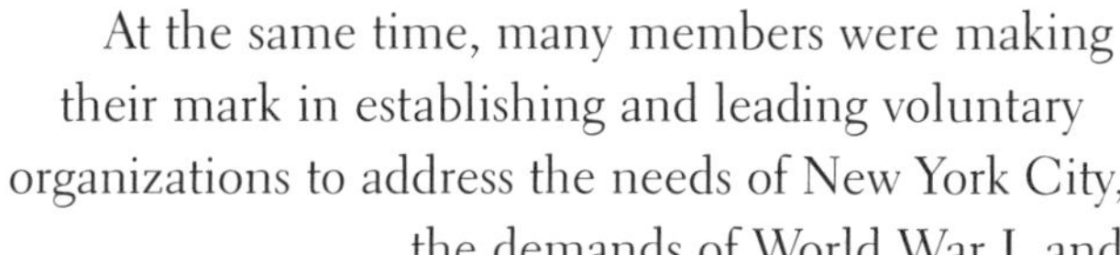

At the same time, many members were making their mark in establishing and leading voluntary organizations to address the needs of New York City, the demands of World War I, and the leading civic issue of the day, female suffrage. Other members played a key role in defining and directing their husbands' philanthropic initiatives. Then, as today, members were of an independent cast of mind, shaping and pursuing their own destiny and seeking the stimulating company of like-minded women.

Reflecting the growing abundance of professional talent and experience among the membership, the Club initiated in 1918 a series of luncheons, at each of which one member shares with other members her professional experience or other interests or activities. These luncheons, weekly during the winter months, are now a prized centerpiece of Club life.

At the same time, the Club's program offerings had expanded to become sufficiently numerous and varied that members in different professions and with diverse talents had the ability, access, and desire to mount a full range of high-quality programs for members and their guests. Thus was born the Arts and Interests Committee, today involving well over 300 members, on a three-year rotating basis, in its sixteen subcommittees, which are responsible for as many different elements of the Club's overall program. This level of member involvement and accountability has to be unique among women's clubs, if not among clubs generally.

In recent years, although the Club maintains a strong base of members across the A&I spectrum of pursuits, the professional balance of the membership has shifted markedly. We now number many lawyers, who revisit our bylaws and rules and monitor compliance in the highly regulated environment in which we operate. At the same time, member MBAs, bankers, investment specialists, economists, and accountants guide our banking relationships, investment portfolio, and multiple forms of insurance coverage. Most significantly, they keep a sharp eye on our financial condition.

Then, new to this era, we have a bevy of computer wizards who are responsible for the Club's hardware and software plus a user-friendly Web site for members. Our ranks also include architects who guard the integrity, inside and out, of our prized building. Other talents are also available for coping with the endless needs of infrastructure and for supplying the managerial expertise and many skills that keep the Clubhouse welcoming, plus the food and wine connoisseurship that gives us pleasure.

While it is fully appropriate, in our centennial year, to recognize and laud the invaluable contributions of members' multiple professional abilities to the vigor and well-being of the Club, we should also celebrate the role of the Club in enriching the lives of these women.

First, there is the pleasure of participating in a worthwhile and collegial endeavor and knowing the satisfaction of a job well done. Also, there is the opportunity to apply one's expertise and experience to new situations and thus expand one's professional competence and reach. Volunteerism in this context embraces these rewards and enhances self-fulfillment. It is most helpful too in honing skills needed to meet the challenges of the often complex philanthropic organizations that many of us also serve.

Then, we know the joy of making new friends to enrich our acquaintance and restock it, as one must, with a younger set. While many members consider themselves nonjoiners, we all find in the Club the sense of well-being promoted by the stimulating company of active and engaged women. The bond of friendship follows easily, underscoring the Club's meaning for us.

Finally, to close on a personal note, I am most grateful to the Club in a way that I never could have imagined when I started out as a new member with a committee assignment that drew on my professional background. Some years later I had the good fortune to meet my future husband (happily, the son of a member) at the Club, at a members dinner dance, on Leap Night! Years of joy followed, enhanced by the pleasure of many shared occasions at the Club and enriched by the friendships each of us had there. Fortunate we all are as members, but none more than I!

CHARLOTTE P. ARMSTRONG

A Clubhouse Fretted in Ironwork

After years of rushing across East Sixty-sixth Street wondering what inspired the airy, delicate tiers of iron balconies on the Club's facade, I decided it was time to consult the standard sources and dig through the Club's Archives. *The AIA Guide to New York City* (2000) lists the Cosmopolitan Club as "one of the northernmost outposts of 'New Orleans' cast iron." Robert A. M. Stern's *Architecture and Urbanism Between the Two World Wars* (1987) describes the Clubhouse as of "Regency design . . . with refreshingly beautiful iron balcony railings and elegantly shaped rooms." The Club's Archives have an abundant trove of newspaper and magazine articles from 1933 soon after the Clubhouse opened. While two of these accounts characterize the new ten-story building as being "cosmopolitan and modern" and as possessing "distinctive modernized classicism," most articles reference its style to the past. One article describes it as "an Italian palazzo," another as harking back to "old New York," and a third as being "Regency in design."

The most detailed description appeared in *Town & Country* magazine. This critic wrote: "It is as though [Thomas Harlan Ellett, the architect] had been to Greece and had become inspired with . . . the uplift of the Doric column. It isn't that he actually uses columns or that he tries, like Thomas Jefferson, to build Greek temples. But he has felt the urge to exalt the commonplaces of living through architectural vision. And he has not shut out the influences of his own time. . . . Mr. Ellett has recalled his old Manhattan and old New Orleans through a series of balconies on the rear of the clubhouse."

"For the posts of the hanging gardens," the critic continued, Ellett "has designed an open grapevine pattern that runs with the optimistic freedom of a Gothic carving." The Sixty-sixth Street facade balconies, he concluded, were not old New York and old New Orleans. Rather, "they are an open, light, and soaring geometric design [that] supports the perpendicularity of the building."

With all these influences in mind, I went outside to study the exterior ironwork. The

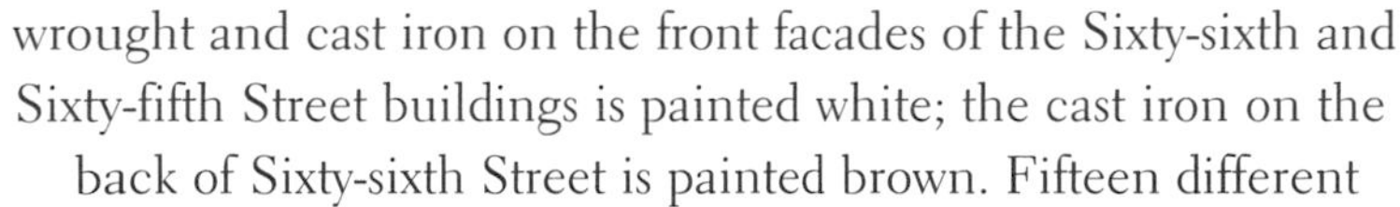

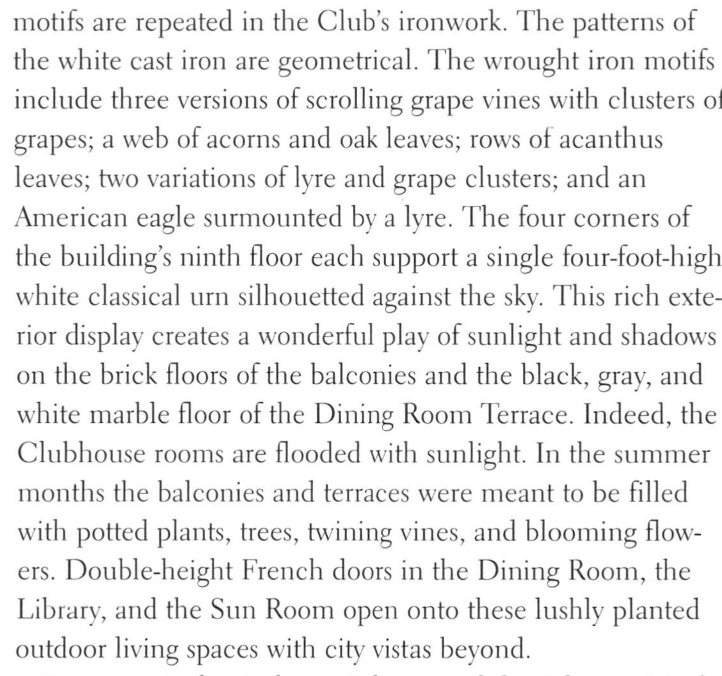

wrought and cast iron on the front facades of the Sixty-sixth and Sixty-fifth Street buildings is painted white; the cast iron on the back of Sixty-sixth Street is painted brown. Fifteen different motifs are repeated in the Club's ironwork. The patterns of the white cast iron are geometrical. The wrought iron motifs include three versions of scrolling grape vines with clusters of grapes; a web of acorns and oak leaves; rows of acanthus leaves; two variations of lyre and grape clusters; and an American eagle surmounted by a lyre. The four corners of the building's ninth floor each support a single four-foot-high white classical urn silhouetted against the sky. This rich exterior display creates a wonderful play of sunlight and shadows on the brick floors of the balconies and the black, gray, and white marble floor of the Dining Room Terrace. Indeed, the Clubhouse rooms are flooded with sunlight. In the summer months the balconies and terraces were meant to be filled with potted plants, trees, twining vines, and blooming flowers. Double-height French doors in the Dining Room, the Library, and the Sun Room open onto these lushly planted outdoor living spaces with city vistas beyond.

Returning to the Archives, I discovered that Eleanor Hardy Platt had chaired the Club's Building Committee. Mrs. Platt was the wife of Charles A. Platt, the architect of the neo-Italian Renaissance style apartment building at 131–135 East Sixty-sixth Street. The Platts were longtime summer residents of the Cornish, New Hampshire, artists' colony where painters, sculptors, writers, lawyers, doctors, and politicians spent their days in the studio and enjoyed theatricals, pageants, and sunsets from their gardens during the evenings. Charles Platt was the architect and landscape designer of nearly a dozen Cornish houses and established the colony's distinctive architectural style.

Thomas Harlan Ellett, the husband of Club member Jane Bigelow Ellett, was a neighbor of the Platts in Cornish. The Iowa-born, University of Pennsylvania–trained architect studied architecture as a fellow at the American Academy in Rome. When Mrs. Platt requested that Ellett reference the Cos Club's Italianate-inspired former home and develop a building that would be "informal, simple, unconventional, [something reflecting] a spirit of good comradeship and a vital interest in the liberal arts," he knew what to do. And he did it well. The Architectural League of New York presented the Gold Medal Award to Ellett for his design of the Cosmopolitan Club, describing it as "a fresh and personal interpretation, beautiful in its simplicity of form and material."

CYNTHIA VAN ALLEN SCHAFFNER

From Generation to Generation

Our family has a long connection to the Club. My grandmother, Jane Tutt Fraser, and my great aunt, Myra R. Tutt, were members, one joining in 1918, the other in 1921. Two aunts, Myra Fraser Martin and Jane Fraser Coleman, as well as cousins, including Ursula Corning, were also longstanding members.

My first remembrance of the Cosmopolitan Club is from 1938 when my mother, Ann Fraser Brewer, took me to Miss Covington's dance class on a Wednesday afternoon after school. The class, held in the Club ballroom, was already under way, boys lined on one side and girls on the other. The girls, mostly taller than the boys, wore white cotton gloves, the piano player pounded out a-one, two, three, and Miss C. called, "Right foot side, left foot back, slide together, slide." The scene appeared strange and terrifying. At thirteen and recently removed from the country where we lived on the edge of marshes with freedom to wander as we chose, I had never encountered such a challenge.

I soon learned more benign aspects of the Club. During the week, I attended the Brearley School and lived with my great-aunt on Park Avenue. The two of us dined weekly at the Club on Thursday, cook's day off. I wore a blue velvet dress and patent leather shoes and we would sit in the Club parlor, my aunt with a glass of dry sherry and I with tomato juice. The Dining Room murals, recently completed by Mr. Cox, were much admired. I spent time trying to figure out the story behind the masks.

In the Club's beauty parlor I had my braids cut off and my first permanent wave. It was a long, daunting process that involved fat curlers attached to wires that hung from the ceiling, a certain amount of hissing steam, and chemical smells. My new hairdo did little to transform me into a city sophisticate. The Club's brand of cold cream, a distinctive pale pink with the horse emblem on the jar, did not endow me with a perfect complexion, but it became a nightly ritual and I remember it with pleasure.

My aunt Myra Martin was a sponsor for the Cosmopolitan Club dances for teenagers. At these gatherings we put to the test the one, two, three steps learned earlier in the ballroom. At first these occasions were, for me, agonizing, but I became inured to them and in fact made friends there with a good number of young New Yorkers. After a dance was over, we were permitted to go to one nightclub, La Rue. It was from that approved venue that I escaped with an equally rebellious boy to explore the downtown scene at the Village Vanguard and Nick's.

The Club continued to be part of my life through my college years. I met friends there, had my hair done, changed clothes to go out for dinner. (How often we changed clothes in those days!) We could get theater or ballet tickets through the Club's secretary and were often supplied with a pair on the aisle at the last minute.

My mother was an active participant in Club happenings, and (I believe) served on the

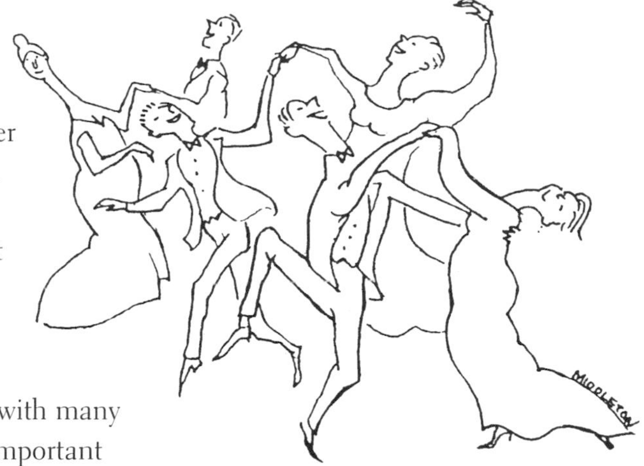

board in the late thirties after we moved from Massachusetts. She attended Member Luncheons and with my father went to Club dances. Under the direction of Ruth Loud, she took part in theatrical performances. I remember the excitement when she and my two aunts created a *tableau vivant* of Sargent's portrait of the three Wyndham sisters.

During the war when my father, along with many men, was overseas, the Club became an important social center where women met to exchange news and share anxieties. My mother worked for the Red Cross, and after a long day visiting the families of soldiers wounded or killed she found the Club a haven where she could relax among friends. In spite of war rationing, the Club kitchen still served good meals. (I think we had to bring ration coupons if we had meat, but I'm not sure.)

After my marriage in 1947 I spent much of the next few decades overseas, but when I visited my parents we often dined at the Club. I never lost touch. When my mother moved to Washington and gave up her New York apartment, I no longer had a place to stay when I was in the city. It was then that I joined the Club as a Nonresident Member. I am now familiar with the cheerful bedrooms, the quiet sanctuary of the Library, and the ease of entertaining guests in the Dining Room. It's good to carry on to another generation the tradition of Club membership.

Ann Brewer Knox

The Cos Club, circa 1971

Back when I was a fifth- and sixth-grader at Spence, we all would line up, washed and brushed, white gloves on our hands, patent leather party shoes shining on our feet, and get ready to enter the grand ballroom of the Cos Club for the Knickerbocker Dancing School classes on Thursday afternoons. All of us girls stood in procession, waiting our turn to shake hands with the ladies who ran the dancing school. Each of them would make sure we said our hellos and our names, and always, a few would nod, "Say hello to your mother for me," or they'd recognize my dad's name from book publishing or from my brother, who was a few years ahead of me at St. Bernard's and had already grown out of this ritual. I loved that moment, of knowing they knew me, or at least some of the people who were part of me, and the knowledge that this was a "family place" made it more fun and somehow less daunting to enter a huge, elegant ballroom with gilded moldings and twenty-five-foot ceilings.

Dancing school was both uncomfortable (you could feel the boys' sweaty, hot palms even through your cotton gloves) and social. The girls bonded over the fact that we were taller by a foot than most of our dance partners. We also recognized one another from playing volleyball and basketball and tennis during school, but when our schools' teams were competing we didn't have a chance to forge friendships. Knickerbocker let us know the boys and the girls our own age, living parallel lives at parallel schools.

What made it fun for me, more than learning the cha cha or the foxtrot, was forging friendships with other girls, some of whose children are now friends with my own. I'm still friends to this day with some of these women who back then were from Brearley and Nightingale, Sacred Heart and Chapin. Now we see each other in and around the Upper East Side as moms and working women in the New York community. Even women I rarely see I consider old pals, and when we spot one another passing on Madison Avenue, we exchange warm waves and a smile, like some secret society of women who will always remember our dancing school days.

The Cos Club is host to many "connecting" events in the little village that is Manhattan. Dancing school is just one way it brings together women and families, younger generations and older, and now my own daughter is one of the white-gloved girls who lines up on Thursday afternoons. When I drop her off or pick her up, I see dozens of other women who were there thirty-five years ago and who now are the moms standing outside with their sons and daughters, and we laugh about how many years have passed but how nothing, really, has changed. That's what I love about the Club. Even now, with its vital speakers programs and its up-to-date program offerings, it's still a port in a storm, a stalwart tradition, of women connecting, taking comfort in each other's company, and being set apart, for a few hours, from the hectic world that lies just outside its doors.

LUCY SCHULTE DANZIGER

Entertainments

In 1962, when I first became a member of our delightful Club, most of my friends were members of the Drama Committee, so that was the committee I soon joined, and I have had the fun of being on it and off it a number of times in the past forty-five years.

In my early years in the Club with a stage and draw curtains, we were able to produce short plays, skits, and musical numbers such as a beautiful costumed rendition of "Brush Up Your Shakespeare" from *Kiss Me, Kate* performed by Ethel Barrymore Colt and Peggy Wood. When the Club celebrated its sixtieth anniversary with a production of *The Chocolate*

Soldier, a Viennese waltz orchestra stayed late into the evening so we could dance to our heart's content after the show.

The Drama Committee was very small in the 1960s. I think it generally had a membership of seven or eight, so we held our meetings in the Skinner Room, which seemed very appropriate, with the inspiring number of plays and skits on its shelves. As most of us were or had been professional actresses, our voices tended to rise, particularly when we were discussing something hilariously funny. Inevitably someone would come across from the main library to ask us to hush, closing the door firmly.

When I became chairman for the first time, I was informed by a former chairman, Ruth Loud, that the Club expected us to produce a gala every other year. Budget need not be restrained, she said, because we would invite other appropriate members of the Arts and Interests Committee to join us and they would contribute from their budget. Then I really got in trouble.

Ruth Loud and I, in 1969, together with other members of the Drama Committee, mounted a full-scale production of *The Chocolate Soldier* together with the Music Committee. We had Charles Dodsley Walker, a celebrated choirmaster, as our music director. The ladies' parts were all performed by Cosmopolitan Club singers, and the gentlemen recruited from the Blue Hill Troupe. Sally Smith, whose husband was singing the male lead, and I did the scenery. With the permission of the House Committee we had hired an artist friend, Donald Tirrell, to paint a glorious mural of the Austrian Alps right on the wall of the alcove in the ballroom, covering it with red balloon curtains for milady's boudoir in the first act. I had spent hours running up the red satin (left over from the circus production of the previous year) on Sally's sewing machine.

My downfall came when we decided to hire a small part of the wonderful Viennese Orchestra from the Ambassador Hotel, making way for a glorious evening but putting us way over budget. As I had, before joining the Club, served successfully as treasurer of the Girl Scout Council of Greater New York for a number of years, my proposer, Harriet Phipps, had put "very good at finance" on my card, which the head of the A&I committee thought was very funny.

Another production in which I was involved was *The Story of the Opera* starring Brenda Forbes and performed with other skits in May 1991. Brenda had performed it originally on Broadway in 1946 in the musical

J.M.

revue *Three to Make Ready.* At the climax of the short play, Brenda as Marilyn, in her enthusiasm as she tells her friend about the story of Wagner's opera *The Valkyrie,* climbs upon a chair in her lovely silver ball gown and grabs the silver cover off the platter that the waiter has just brought in, releasing a wave of hot steam produced by a smoke machine. With our wonderful light board we were able to infuse the stage with a red glow while Brenda, at the top of her lungs, sang "Give me fire! Fire! Fire!!!" At this point our poor manager, Rita Evans, walked into the ballroom from the pantry and nearly had a heart attack, thinking the Club was on fire.

These are just some of the fun things in which I have been involved at the Club over the past forty-five years and only a few of the delightful people I have had the honor of working with.

ESTHER LEEMING TUTTLE

Things My Mother Taught Me

I attended an all boys' school—that is, one that had remained so until 1974, four years before my matriculation. I also attended an all men's college—that is, all male until 1977, five years before my matriculation. Though the student bodies were no longer all male, both institutions retained their maleness long after becoming coeducational. So it was with great excitement that I became a member of the Cosmopolitan Club in 2000, shortly after the birth of my son. At age thirty-six, I had matriculated into my own midlife version of an all women's college, and not a moment too soon. I immediately set out to join the Younger Members Committee and, three years later, the Art Committee; both have been cornerstones for forming enjoyable and lasting friendships.

This past winter, following our monthly Thursday Art Committee meeting, a group of eight retired to the Members Dining Room to relish a famous Cos Club cheese soufflé. Our table's discussion turned toward memories of "things my mother taught me." One lively and accomplished woman in her eighties, with a distinguished career in the arts, said that her mother had bestowed these two gems: "Never eat smoked salmon at a cocktail party" and "Never expose the décolletage to the sun."

A riotous and lengthy conversation ensued about the importance of fresh breath. After all, who knows whom one might meet at any given moment in New

York, and is a whiff of salmon breath really the best first impression? As for the décolletage, I know we have all been at the beach and seen the damage the sun can do. Why, just this past Labor Day, I saw a woman . . . Well, suffice it to say, her mother never told her to keep out of the sun!

I was at first slightly self-conscious to share my pieces of maternal wisdom, for I too had been taught many important lessons by my mother. Two memorable dictums popped into my head immediately. When my sister, Sarah, and I were teenagers at boarding school in the 1970s, my mother had advised: "If you are going to have sex, come home and do it in the guest bedroom and *always* use contraceptives" and "If you are going to smoke pot, do it in the kitchen so the house won't burn down."

My mother assumed (*not necessarily correctly*) that her daughters would experiment, and she intended to protect us—not from the experiences of young adulthood, but from the consequences that could ensue (unplanned pregnancy, expulsion from school, accidental fire). Much like the mother of my Art Committee colleague, my mother four decades later cared deeply about her daughters' lives and set about instilling a sense of responsibility toward our bodies and ourselves. While the times had certainly changed, the maternal advice remained constant.

Our conversation took many twists and turns, and Saul, our ever-gracious server, commented that he had never seen such a raucous bunch at lunch. Most notable were the laughter and the open and trusting way that each woman at the table shared her experiences with her fellow Club members. This conversation has stayed with me for months. It speaks to friendship among women at the Club and the warm, honest, intergenerational dialogue that occurs here. Spanning more than forty years in age, we all had something real and important to share. The sharing brought laughter, the laughter brought friendship, and friendship is what makes the Cos Club the Cos Club.

REBECCA ABRAMS

My Tea

Late in 2003, I was proposed as a member of the Cosmopolitan Club and told that to be admitted I needed to attend a Membership Committee tea. My only knowledge of the organization was gleaned from being a guest at the 2000 New Year's Eve gala and during a reading of a book I wrote. Essentially, I knew nothing—nothing except for my general knowledge of clubs.

Any adult club that isn't devoted to one particular activity, such as macramé, gardening, or Elvis fandom, always makes me a little suspicious. Why is the membership limited? What are they trying to hide? And more importantly, what weird rites, what cloak-and-dagger activities are required for initiation?

My imagination ran wild. What if the Cos Club was connected to the medieval Knights Templar? Would I have to ransack Egyptian tombs, or at the very least the Temple of Dendur? Maybe it was a chapter of Skull and Bones and I would be compelled to lie in a coffin in total darkness without cable or room service. Perhaps the Cos was more hard-core and ventured into gang activities, forcing new initiates to participate in drive-by posture corrections. I needed to know.

I asked everyone I met who belonged to the Cos about this sinister-sounding tea. They all had the same response: "It's no big deal. It's just the committee members trying to get to know more about you." Their well-crafted lies led me to the New York Public Library where I delved into a thorough and somewhat surprising research project to uncover the truth about the initiation practices of the club.

Sifting through miles of microfiche, I arrived at a most sobering news report dated April 20, 1966. Apparently the Board of Governors of our august club in that particular year dictated that new initiates were required to help the most recent members of the Knickerbocker Club stage a panty raid at the Colony Club. The prank failed when one member, buckling under the combined weight of so many undergarments, fell from her makeshift ladder and tumbled onto a balcony garden somewhere on Sixty-second Street, flattening a row of rare Abyssinian tulips right in front of the shocked, trowel-wielding resident.

To say that the next few days were tense at 122 East Sixty-sixth is an understatement. A citywide brouhaha was threatening to erupt at any minute. However, never short on pluck, the Cos women of the Mischief and Mayhem Committee (since redubbed Younger Members) took action. During a standoff with the police they demanded to speak with Mayor Lindsay. Once Lindsay entered the building, the Hospitality Committee went to work. Opening up the finest Bordeaux in the cellar, they treated him to our outstanding chef's mouth-watering delicacies. They read passages from the many books and periodicals that bear the names of Cosmopolitan women, as authors and as subjects. They brought in many accomplished members to enlighten him on just as many topics. They taught him French (intermediate) and yoga.

As the evening built to a crescendo, they brought out the coup de grâce: a musical comedy about the city council starring the lovely and talented members of the Drama Committee. Enjoying himself immensely, Lindsay seemed to be teetering off his stated position against the Club. The Public Interests Committee rightly determined that this was the moment to seal the deal. They rushed to the bartender and asked him to invent a concoction that was as sweet, snappy, and intoxicating as the members. Mixing a few choice ingredients in a gleaming silver shaker, he masterfully strained a glistening ruby liquid into a chilled martini glass that they then presented to the mayor. Thus the Cosmopolitan cocktail was born and the Cosmopolitan Club was saved.

Despite their success, the members preferred not to memorialize the event; in fact, they chose to bury it. For the next twenty years all Cosmopolitan Club women were sworn to secrecy, which is why if you ask any of our longtime members about the tomfoolery of that warm April night, they will look at you quizzically and swear they have no idea what you're talking about.

So on a snowy January day I attended my tea, somewhat anxiously as I knew not what sort of secret rituals would be forced upon me. To my surprise, the room was well lit and the only oddity was the way each interviewer switched from one prospective member to another with the timed precision of a chess match clock.

In the end, it was, in fact, no big deal, just committee members trying to get to know more about me. Although I was relieved, I was a tad disappointed—that is, until I attended my first event as a full-fledged member. Sitting comfortably in the dining room, I realized that, like John Lindsay forty years before, I was enjoying excellent food and wine and the delightful company of some of the most interesting women in New York.

SUSAN STEVENSON BOROWITZ

Macaroons and Cheese Soufflés

Within a week of becoming chairperson of the Food Committee several years ago, I was told that certain customs were sacrosanct. That would present no problem, I felt sure, and indeed the two bedrocks of food tradition at the Cosmopolitan Club proved to be delightful: macaroons and cheese soufflé. I wouldn't have changed either one of them, even if it had cost me my toque. Macaroons were served after every meal, whether one had ordered dessert or not. A favorite after-dinner gambit went: "I'm not sure these macaroons are as soft as they used to be. What do you think?" Someone at the table invariably answered, "Oh, they're not nearly as good as they once were." And so it went through the years even though the recipe was unchanged. Macaroons are beloved at other New York clubs, too. The Century Association is equally proud of theirs, and I once proposed that we have a macaroon bakeoff at some teatime, a cookie contest between two redoubtable institutions. I was unpersuasive and it never took place, although we would have won in a bite.

Cheese soufflés were available, and delectable, every Thursday at lunch. But they were not on the menu, and it was only when one saw these quivering towers of aromatic froth arriving, seemingly unbidden, at neighboring tables that one began to realize one was missing something. Not

J·M

to worry—many Thursdays lay ahead. The secrecy rule was maintained in the vain hope that the kitchen would not be overwhelmed. But the kitchen never disappointed even after the secret was out and cheese soufflés were ordered by *every* table, *every* Thursday.

In that same first week on the Food Committee there was an event of consequence. The longtime chef quit. I tell myself this was not due to my arrival as we had yet to meet. But perhaps he had read my cookbook and decided the kitchen was too hot for both of us. At any rate, a number of members and staff were soon conducting interviews and tastings with prospective chefs on an almost daily basis. We settled on a young Frenchman whose presentation was outstanding. However, as soon as he was behind the stove he began suggesting such Gallic niceties as squirrel, brains, and various other entrails and organs. Had we all been deluded? No, not at all. In no time he understood our members and our members loved his style. It wasn't long before one told me in a confessional tone, "My husband would never eat here. Now he says it's the best French restaurant in New York." What a delicious moment. I still savor it.

ELEANOR MACKENZIE GRAVES

A Long Journey

When I became a member of the Cosmopolitan Club, in 1996, long after I had emigrated from Czechoslovakia to the United States, I felt myself to be a true New Yorker and an American. This wonderful organization introduced me to a form of community that I was unfamiliar with—there was no "club culture" in my birthplace. In fact, when my husband, Jan, and I boarded a plane one cold, sunny February day in 1965, officially becoming immigrants, I had no sense of a communal culture at all.

By that time I realized I was not leaving behind much of anything. Continuous political upheavals had already destroyed a long-established society; social contacts had crumbled in its wake, and life had become increasingly difficult. It had become unwise to trust anybody; the norm was to see the faces of people—even those one knew well—turn blank, in self-preservation. It was safer to turn inward, to keep one's thoughts and opinions to oneself.

This way of life infiltrated even the family structure. My family had grown apart. By the time my mother, the spiritual center of our family, died, we had lost all our privileges and most of our comforts. Thus, the promises my two brothers and I made to each other after my mother's funeral, to stay together and help each other, did not hold fast. My older brother, a physician, soon went to France to study and then moved to America. And my father? He was there, but not really present. Certainly he was not used to taking care of children, except to monitor our progress at school. Today, with the clarity only hindsight brings, I understand that he was struggling to cope with his own sorrow. Not only had he lost his wife, this proud and accomplished man had also lost his responsible position in education and worked at menial jobs.

All of this made departure easier. I was not leaving a supportive family structure or a network of close friends, and I no longer had strong feelings of national belonging. Rather quickly, my thoughts turned to a day I had lived a thousand times in my imagination. Now, I was sitting on a plane, clutching my briefcase, which held the all-important envelope containing our immigration documents, and hoping we had all we needed to pass "inspection" in New York. I knew the city only from photographs, books, and stories, so even as we drew closer it seemed mysterious, exciting, and enticing.

Then, suddenly, we were at Kennedy Airport. Breaths held, we passed through immigration. My older brother was there to meet us, though we hardly recognized each other after ten years. But I had no time to think about that. Before I knew it, there it was, in front of me: the Manhattan skyline, gleaming in the sunny winter afternoon, a magic floating island of architectural madness, full of promise and opportunities. I still think of this moment, this first sight of the great metropolis, every day, and remember wondering if I would ever be able to blend into this landscape.

I struggled at first, seeming to live two lives. In my sleep, dreams took me back to my birthplace. In the morning, I woke to dislocation and readjustment. I could not even understand the weather report! How would I ever learn how to live and work in this place? My husband and I made a conscious decision to adjust and find ways to integrate into our new homeland.

For me, that meant finding a place in the art world. Art history, my profession, would not, on the face of it, seem the most practical field for an immigrant. Yet within months I had found my professional home, the Metropolitan Museum of Art, where I worked happily for more than three decades. My years there were instrumental in shaping my personal life as well as my professional development. The intellectual environment of that great institution enabled me to blend the culture of my past with the one I found here.

At the museum I met colleagues who were members of the Cosmopolitan Club and its arts program. Through their gracious support, I became a member of the Club, and its cultural events and civilized facilities expanded my feeling of belonging. Joining the Club also enabled me to spread my professional wings outside the museum. From 2000 to 2003, I was a member of the Club's Art Committee.

My husband and I never forget how very lucky we were to come here, where we have felt welcomed to practice our professions and form new social ties. When I retrace the steps that took me from the day we arrived to now, I count membership in the Cosmopolitan Club as an important part of the journey.

MARICA VILCEK

The Arts in the Early Years at the Cos Club

Several years ago, in the course of researching an article about Abby Aldrich Rockefeller for *Antiques* magazine, I discovered that she was one of the founding members of our Club. My primary interest in Mrs. Rockefeller at the time was her role as a founder of another New York institution, the Museum of Modern Art. When I was asked to write this essay for the centennial book, I was reminded of the wonderful correspondence between Mrs. Rockefeller and her friends who so boldly wanted the world to understand the art of their time. As I began to read through the archives of the Club to learn about the early membership, I found a number of familiar names and encountered dozens of other women who were equally fascinating. Alas, in the interest of brevity, I couldn't write about them all. What follows is only a sampling.

When the Cosmopolitan Club was founded, society, and especially the role of women, was rapidly changing. The first generation of members was eager to understand this new world. Intellectually curious and eager to learn, these intrepid women sought the companionship of their peers. They chose to present exhibitions and lectures on the arts that focused primarily on what was current. From Vita Sackville-West's lecture "The Modern Spirit in Literature" to Salvador Dalí's "Le Surréalisme de Vermeer de Delft," the speakers and their subjects were erudite, timely, and occasionally controversial. Among the writers and musicians who came to the Club to talk about their work were W. H. Auden, Nadia Boulanger, Robert Frost, John Galsworthy, Paul Hindemith, Carl Sandburg, Virgil Thomson, and Elinor Wylie.

That first generation of members included an astonishing number of artists, collectors, critics, art educators, and curators. These professional women and gifted amateurs created a challenging program of art exhibitions and lectures and set a standard of excellence that the Club has sought to maintain ever since. Through their satirical cartoons of women and contemporary life published in the *New Yorker* and elsewhere, artist members such as Helen Hokinson (1893–1949), Peggy Bacon (1895–1987), and Mary Petty (1899–1976) helped keep the membership from taking themselves too seriously.

In 1914, Cecilia Beaux (1855–1942) joined the Committee on Art and organized an exhibition of her own work. William Merritt Chase referred to Beaux as "not only the greatest woman painter, but the best that has ever lived." She was the first woman to teach at the Pennsylvania Academy, and she won gold medals at the Carnegie International and the Paris Exposition. That same year, Isabel McIlwaine Manship organized an exhibition of her husband's sculpture. Recently awarded the Prix de Rome, Paul Manship had returned from Italy with a body of new work characterized by elongated figures that anticipated Art Deco and found a wide audience.

The following year, Amy Lowell presented a talk entitled "The New Manner in Modern Poetry," and Messrs. Durand-Ruel lent paintings by Monet, Pissarro, Renoir, and Sisley for exhibition and probable sale.

In 1916, Frederick James Gregg, who masterminded the publicity for the Armory Show that had taken New York by storm only three years earlier and who wrote the preface for the catalogue, gave a talk entitled "The Paradox of Art." Frank Crowninshield, the editor of *Vanity Fair,* took part in "The New Magazine Writing," a symposium held at the Club focusing on modern life. Shortly after being named editor and drama critic of *The Dial* in 1922, American cultural critic Gilbert Seldes spoke at the Club about the magazine.

In December 1917, the exhibition "Modern Paintings" was held at the Club and included a still life modeled in reinforced concrete by Pablo Picasso. This important early exhibition of modern art, one of the first in the United States to include Picasso's relief sculpture, was reviewed in *American Art News.* Artists in the show included Georges Braque, André Derain, Man Ray, Diego Rivera, Joseph Stella, and others whose work is now widely recognized. The artist Katherine Dreier (1877–1952) joined the Club that year. Several years later she founded the Société Anonyme with Marcel Duchamp to promote modern art. Dreier gave several Member Luncheon talks, including, in 1927, "What About Modern Art?"

Although not all early lectures and activities are accounted for, the Archives contain tantalizing invitations to outside events as well as early written memoirs revealing the lively and provocative programs and discussions at the Club. Anne Kidder Wilson, wife of noted scientist Edmund B. Wilson, wrote in "A Bird's Eye View from 1918" that the membership spent "one deeply interested afternoon at Miss Helen Frick's invitation, at the opening of her Frick Art Reference Library." Josephine Pomeroy Hendrick, chair of the Arts and Interests Committee, bemoaned her small budget for speakers, writing that to obtain "popular speakers" on the arts, music, literature, drama, and public affairs, one had to pay a fee, and her budget was only $800.

J.M.

Among the Club's early members were collectors of modern art, among whom were the trio of women who helped found the Museum of Modern Art: Lillie P. Bliss (1864–1931), Abby Aldrich Rockefeller (1874–1948), and Mary Quinn Sullivan (1877–1939). They joined Adele Herter (1869–1946), an artist and collector who had married into the famous Herter family of designers; Rue Winterbotham Carpenter (1879–1931), the driving force behind the progressive Arts Club of Chicago; and Mabel Choate (1870–1958) and her Boston cousin Sarah Choate Sears (1858–1935), patrons and collectors with a deep interest in contemporary art. Agnes Ernst Meyer (1887–1970), mother of Katherine Graham and an early patron and colleague of both Alfred Stieglitz and Marius de Zayas, was another member, as were Theodate Pope (1867–1946), the pioneering architect and collector who in conjunction with McKim, Mead & White designed Hillstead, a family house in Farmington, Connecticut, that evolved into a museum for her family's collection, and Lydia Winston Malbin (1897–1989), a pioneering Detroit collector of Italian Futurist art.

Continuing this impressive tradition, subsequent generations of collectors joined the Club, including two presidents of the Board of Trustees of MoMA, Elizabeth Bliss Parkinson Cobb (1907–2001) and Blanchette Hooker Rockefeller (1909–1992); Sally Wile Ganz (1912–1997), who with her husband, Victor, collected Picasso and Matisse deeply and with discernment; Susan Morse Hilles (1905–2002), the first woman to serve as a trustee at the Boston Athenaeum; and Eloise O'Mara Spaeth (1902–1998), founder of the Guild Hall Museum in Easthampton.

The first generation of professional women working in the arts were also represented in the Club's membership. They included Helen Appleton Read (1874–1974), the art critic for the *Brooklyn Daily Eagle* who championed contemporary art, and Elisabeth Luthar Cary (1867–1936), the art critic for the *New York Times* and author of thirteen books on art and American literature. Juliana Rieser Force (1876–1948), the first director of the Whitney Museum, joined the Club, undoubtedly encouraged by Gertrude Vanderbilt Whitney (1875–1942), artist, collector, founder of the Whitney, and briefly a member. Agnes Mongan (1905–1996), the first female curator at the Fogg Art Museum, joined, as did author and educator Margaret Scolari Barr (1901–1987), the wife of Alfred Barr, the founding director of MoMA with whom she worked on many projects. *New York Times* art and architecture critic Aline Saarinen (1914–1972), the first woman to head an overseas news bureau (Paris) and author of *The Proud Possessors*, which chronicled the rise of American art collectors, was another member.

In 1928, the Club mounted an exhibition of bronze sculpture by Aristide Maillol, presumably lent by members. There was also an exhibition of paintings by Childe Hassam organized by his wife, Maude Doane Hassam, who was a member.

The following year, Dudensing Galleries lent an exhibition of contemporary artists, presumably for sale, and Mrs. Samuel Lewisohn, whose daughters were members, lent paintings by Gauguin, Matisse, Modigliani, Picasso, and Redon from her collection, now in the

Metropolitan Museum of Art. Also in 1929, the Downtown Gallery mounted a show of contemporary American artists Alexander Brook and Glenn Coleman. The artist and member Hildreth Meière (1892–1961) exhibited cartoons for her murals. Meière later designed the Art Deco plaques on the exterior of Radio City Music Hall and stained glass windows for St. Bartholomew's Church and served as president of the National Society of Mural Painters.

Other prominent artist members included Enid Yandell (1871–1934), who sculpted the caryatids for the woman's pavilion of the 1893 Chicago World Columbian Exposition; Alice Boughton (1866–1943), a photographer who worked as an assistant in Gertrude Kasebier's studio and was later part of Stieglitz's Photo-Secessionist circle; Anna Vaughn Hyatt Huntington (1876–1973), a sculptor who won the purple rosette of the French government and was made a chevalier of the Légion d'Honneur for her equestrian group, *Joan of Arc*; and Isabel Bishop (1902–1988), a figurative artist whose skills as a draftsman enabled her to teach widely. She was the first woman to hold an executive position in the National Institute of Arts and Letters.

This rich tradition of excellence in the arts continues at the Club with a membership of artists, educators, collectors, writers, and museum directors too numerous to list. But the early standards set by the first generation of members speak to a common concern: distinction.

WENDY JEFFERS

Reflections on Being a Member of the Cosmopolitan Club

Joining the Cosmopolitan Club was an unanticipated part of my life in New York City, and it was an unexpected pleasure that the Club became important to me.

I moved here to take a job. New York was where I'd intended to move after college. Despite a twenty-year detour through New Orleans and Washington, D.C., I knew New York well and had many friends and even family here. As president of a national and international NGO, I knew I would be busy and travel a lot and might not even have time for the New York I already knew and loved.

I had seldom ventured into women's clubs. My mother had made me a life member of Hadassah and the National Council of Jewish Women, a sort of rite of passage, and I'd enjoyed informal groups of women who gathered at dinner every few weeks to exchange life's stories. But a club, a place with an actual structure and formal meeting ground, was foreign to me. It felt mysterious and like the type of place that I had been more excluded from than invited into—and that either as a woman in some cases or as a Jew in others, I would not be welcome.

It was one of my board members who suggested proposing me. She described the Cosmopolitan Club as the thinking women's club. Besides pleasing her, my real thought was that joining might show me a part of New York very different from the rest of my life. What I did not expect was that I would grow to love the Cosmopolitan Club, feel it was my slice of life, my home, and find some of my closest friends in its midst. At first I felt conscious of how to be the best Club member, how to fit in. Now I feel as though it is a community that, with friends across the generations, we shape into something we are all proud of.

Soon after I joined, I was asked to serve on the Younger Members Committee. I was surprised that the committee chair knew my name, and her invitation gave me a feeling of belonging. This group showed me that the Cos offered much of what I'd found important in the informal groups that had inspired me to write a book celebrating women's groups, *Girls' Night Out.* Like them, the Cos provides a sense of community and even of family. It offers an anchor in the figurative sense of something one can count on, but also an anchor with physicality to it, a place that is warm and inviting. Having this anchor and feeling a part of a distinguished institution gives me a certain confidence, and even more, empowerment.

Like its building, the Club endures. As my coauthor and I say about women's groups, "It offers a sense of rootedness, a common body of experience and knowledge, a sense of continuity." I may not see my Cos Club friends often, but I know I can count on them. It is also an investment in my future, for what I can learn from others about how to make the next stages of my life as meaningful as possible.

The Club provides a women's network that suggests the power of women to change and better the world. Our programs are my own mini university of sorts, exposing me to ideas and issues that expand my world and suggest ways I can take action. When I have been passionate about a cause, I have been able to invite the women of the Club to learn with me and to care. This was particularly true after Hurricane Katrina. The Club was a venue for the release of Doug Brinkley's best-selling portrait of the impact of the disaster. Later, I would use the Library to host an event for Eve Ensler's *Katrina Monologues: Swimming Upstream.*

I recently went to the younger members' Library dinner. The logs in the fireplace were burning, each table was set with a special decor, and books surrounded us. The lights of the city shone just beyond the terrace. I remembered my first library dinner when I'd been on my best behavior to be sure I could continue to "belong." This time, I felt at home as I visited with friends. We picked up where we had left off. My membership had shifted from a sense of "me belonging to it" to "it belonging to me."

TAMARA KREININ

From Being "Ladies" to Being "Women"

When I was born, women did not yet have the vote. Now, as I write, we have a woman running for President. The century just passed has produced more changes for women than any in history. And the Cosmopolitan Club has valiantly kept up. If there's a single word to describe us, it is *adaptability*. If there is a single phrase, it is that we have moved from being ladies to being women.

Women can be frivolous when the mood is upon us, but basically we are serious as we face the twenty-first century with its unprecedented dangers and opportunities. In more than one sense, we are now wearing pants.

Our professional involvements still include volunteerism (one of our members, Ellen Sulzberger Straus, coined the term "professional volunteer"), and we still engage in artistic endeavors, whether literary or musical or visual, but we have also advanced ourselves in the no-nonsense worlds of law and medicine, finance and business. We not only know, as our mothers possibly did not, what CEO stands for, some of us have attained that lofty status. For many of us the bottom line is now connected with affordability, not simply the lowest entry in a drawing or painting.

What is riveting to me is the parallel between the benefits from being a modern woman and those of aging. In both instances we feel liberated. We are freer with our opinions, more courageous in our stances, attentive to but not limited by what other people think. Though we don't "let it all hang out," we are no longer bound by the many former reticences and fierce guardings of privacy. When we were young—and not terribly interesting—we spent virtually full-time thinking about ourselves. How were we coming across? Were the seams in our stockings straight? Did we say or do something wrong? Yet now that some of us are old—and far more interesting—we go for hours without thinking of ourselves at all. We have too much of greater importance to pay attention to, including the future of the planet and the nation, our city and even our Club.

Why did I join the Cos, to begin with? In part because some old friends were members. I had known Hilda Reis Bijur and Marjorie Lewisohn since kindergarten in Lincoln School in 1923. But mostly I joined because I needed a home away from home. I live in Riverdale and was at a loss for a place to go, say, between the ending of lunch in Manhattan and the beginning of a later engagement. How blessed to be able to retire to the Club Library in an

easy chair or even to sneak into one of the back rooms on the eighth floor and lie down on the carpet to rest my back. The staff is remarkable, not only for their courtesy and apparent joy at our being there, but for their continuity. From the doorman who greets us to the waitresses who feed and water us to the telephone guarders who give us change for parking meters, there always seems to be a face that is familiar.

When I joined the Cos in 1983, most members were WASPs, with a few Catholics thrown into the mix and even fewer Jews. Now we are a veritable rainbow of women, domestic and foreign, ranging in age from our twenties to our nineties, with widely varying backgrounds and proclivities.

The Cos Club's inclusiveness, however, does not apply to men—and, to my knowledge, none of our members wants it to. New York is host to plenty of clubs that admit only men. In my view, both kinds of club are valuable, those for women and those for men.

A club like ours is the perfect setting for nurturing old friendships and establishing new ones either at lunch or tea, drinks or dinner, or attendance at an event. I have yet to sit next to a stranger at our Club who didn't have something interesting to say. Nor is there any longer a condescension between generations. The new egalitarianism is symbolized by everyone using first names on first acquaintance. As for clothing these days, the preference seems to remain for classic rather than up-to-the-minute fashionable—and all generations now wear comfortable shoes.

Lunch may be briefer than formerly because time is so important to working people, but it can still include intimate exchanges. What is missing are the several drinks that used to accompany some lunches. Too many of us need to be able to think clearly in the afternoon as well as the morning. Also we are far more aware of the state of our bodies than many members used to be. We watch our calories or we run or we work out. Our little old ladies in tennis shoes may mask whizbangs on the court. Today, when we older members pass a mirror, we no longer avert our eyes, we merely stick out our tongues.

As for feminism, we range from activists to simple enjoyers of its benefits.

Sometimes the degree of choice before us is awesome, but we have learned that making up our minds, though possibly the hardest work in the world, is worth it. The choice is ours. We serve diligently on one of the Club's committees or we take a free ride for a number of years. We stay home and care for our babies—and, more and more, our grandbabies—or we edge men aside in the big bad world. Whatever we do, our Club is our refuge. We don't open our briefcases in the Lounge, but we open our hearts to one another. We act like the survivors of change that we are, and we help each other decide which further changes to adapt to and which to thumb our noses at.

JUNE BINGHAM

June Rossbach Bingham Birge, the noted biographer and playwright, died August 21, 2007. She generously wrote this essay for the centennial book knowing that she would not be with us to celebrate.

The Cos at 100

photographs by Lindsay Brice

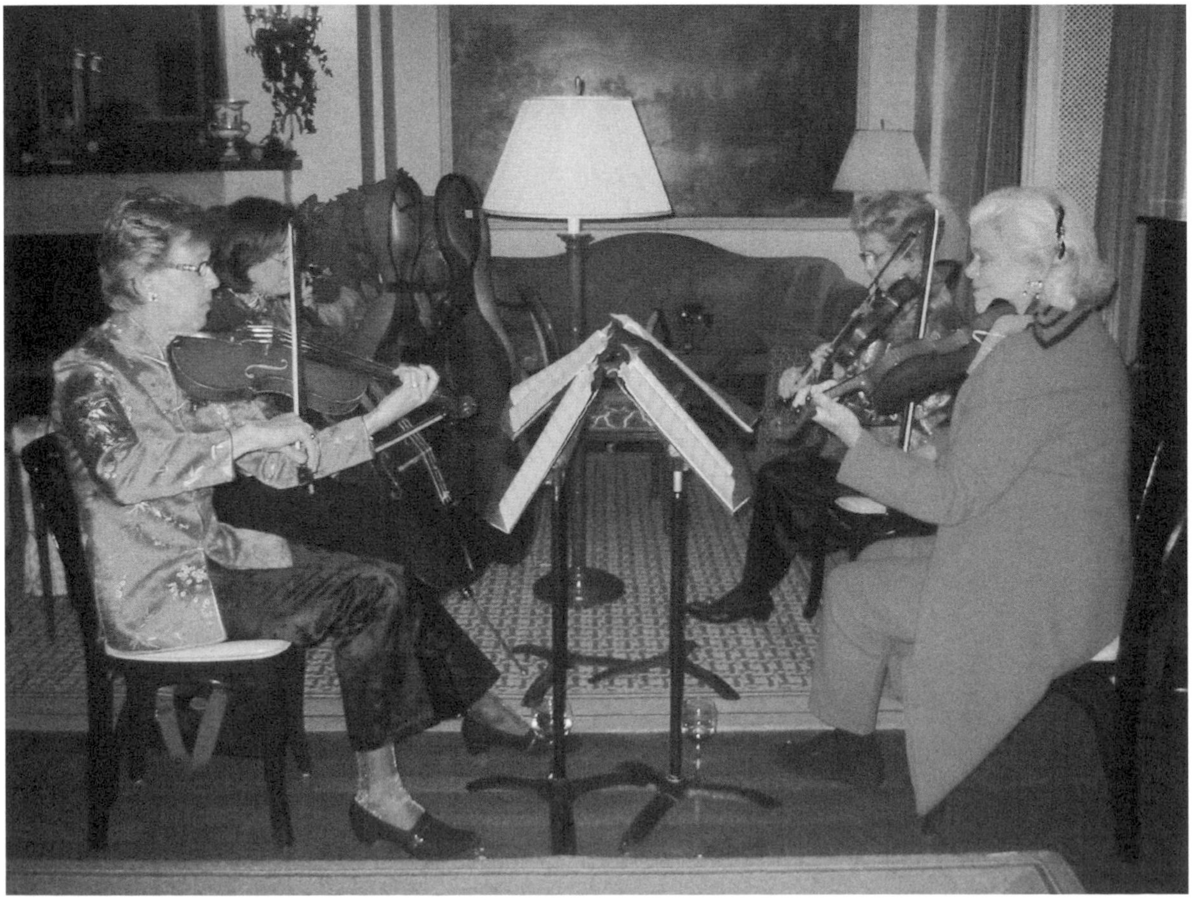

"The nominating committee recommends that we reëlect all of the present officers, as we still have on hand a very large quantity of stationery with their names on it."

An original cartoon by Helen Hokinson from the Club Archives.

Board of Governors 2008–2009

Standing, left to right: Edith Greenwood, Victoria K. Larson, Laura H. Conley, Claudia S. Plottel, Anne W. McIlvaine, Joan Carvo, Anastasia Pappas Polimeni, JoAnn P. Goodspeed, Louise M. Braverman. Seated, left to right: Elizabeth Beim, Helene M. Weld, Molly O. Parkinson, Ann B. Lane, Anne W. Evans, Anne G. B. Grew. Absent: Stuart U. Buice, Andi deF. Emerson, Susan K. Montgomery.

The Opening Celebration of the Centennial on January 22, 2009, honored Presidents Emeritae. Standing, left to right: JoAnn Sawyer Delafield, Doris Halaby, Janet Rodes Hester, Carey French Millard, Sally Thackston Butler, Molly O. Parkinson (outgoing President). Seated, left to right: Rebecca Jackson Sargent, Charlotte P. Armstrong, Dorothea Kidder Smith, Elizabeth H. Gaillard, Hilda Reis Bijur.

Former Presidents

Helen Gilman Brown, 1911–1914
Laura Billings Lee, 1914–1919
Florence M. Marshall, 1919–1922
Anne Kidder Wilson, 1922–1925
Maud Durbin Skinner, 1925–1928
Alice Kirkham Lord, 1928–1931
Alida Leese Milliken, 1931–1932
Rosamond Gilder, 1932–1933
Agnes Brown Leach, 1933–1937
Dorothy Kidder Riggs, 1937–1940
Alice Bacon Woolsey, 1940–1946
Mary Ballard Duryee, 1946–1949
Ruth Davis Steinway, 1949–1952
Katharine Lord Mali, 1952–1955
Frederica Pisek Barach Barbour, 1955–1958
Elizabeth Braley Dewey, 1958–1961
Mary St. John Villard, 1961–1964
Ethel Halsey Blum, 1964–1967
Margaret Ogden, 1967–1970
Elizabeth H. Gaillard, 1970–1973
Elizabeth M. Riley, 1973–1976
Katherine Miller Scott, 1976–1979
Hilda Reis Bijur, 1979–1982
Dorothea Kidder Smith, 1982–1985
JoAnn Sawyer Delafield, 1985–1988
Rebecca Jackson Sargent, 1988–1991
Doris Halaby, 1991–1994
Carey French Millard, 1994–1997
Janet Rodes Hester, 1997–2000
Sally Thackston Butler, 2000–2003
Charlotte P. Armstrong, 2003–2006
Molly O. Parkinson, 2006–2009

The staff of the Cosmopolitan Club.

Acknowledgments

This book could not have been produced without the assistance and support of many members of the Cosmopolitan Club. First and foremost, of course, are Molly O. Parkinson, our President, and the Board of Governors.

Kitty Benton and Laura Huizinga Conley, of the Centennial Committee, acted in an advisory capacity, ensuring that this history would complement other celebrations planned for the centennial year and be an appropriate tribute to our past and present.

Members of the Archives Committee, Gabrielle McVeigh Cassou, Yasmine Ergas, Willa Hutner, and Estelle Nicki Tanner, helped to envision the form the book might take and in early planning. The centennial history project moved forward after Archives member Sandy Alcott Shalleck designed an elegant, illustrated, sample chapter that was submitted to the Board of Governors for consideration and won approval.

Lucienne Schupf Bloch, author of the historical narrative, then skillfully transformed a mass of archival research into an entertaining and authoritative narrative for which we are profoundly appreciative and grateful. Our essayists, Rebecca Abrams, Charlotte P. Armstrong, June Bingham, Susan Stevenson Borowitz, Jill Ker Conway, Lucy Schulte Danziger, Eleanor MacKenzie Graves, Evelyn J. Halpert, Wendy Jeffers, Ann Brewer Knox, Tamara Kreinin, Esther Leeming Tuttle, and Marica Vilcek, thoughtfully responded to our request for individual points of view, producing a variety of charming and informative accounts. Embellishing the essays are the line drawings of Joan Middleton, who was kind enough to draw several especially for this work. Lindsay Brice, Caroline Brown, and Matthew Mauro, highly skilled photographers, documented the Club's present-day vibrancy, rounding out our rich selection of images from the past.

Other Club members who helpfully provided details for the historical research or gave other assistance were Christina Lang Assael, Elizabeth Artz Beim, Sally Thackston Butler, Rita Chen Chu, Frances Ferry Dennison, Louise Meière Dunn, Anne Wilson Evans, Ann Bollman Goldsmith, Jo Ann P. Goodspeed, Ann Gano Bailey Grew, Edna Perkel Gurewitsch, Chantal Leroy Hodges, Holly Stevenson Hunt, Shirley Dawson Kirkland, Susan Kingsbury Montgomery, Janet M. Offensend, Georgia Urbano Raysman, Elizabeth Rees, Rona Kaplan Roob, Julia C. Schieffelin, Dorothea Kidder Smith, and Mary Stuhr Yellen.

Staff members, always ready to offer their aid for Club enterprises, were particularly generous in providing us with assistance, information, and advice. In this regard, special thanks go to General Manager Christian Dewailly, and to current and former staff members Susan

Bonds, Marina Costake, Rita Evans, Jaclyn Flynn, Antoinette Grando, Pina Mikulian, William R. Reader, and Marge Shiroky. Alice Dunn, as Club librarian and an eighth-floor neighbor of the Archives, was a constant source of cheerful encouragement of our work.

Finally, our thanks go to Aaron Tilford and Ron Gordon of The Oliphant Press not only for their professional competence in designing and printing our book but for their sensitivity in working with the members of the Centennial Book Committee to satisfy the many concerns about what should finally appear in these pages.

Sophia Duckworth Schachter
Caroline Fraser Zinsser
Cynthia Van Allen Schaffner

Photography Credits

All illustrations are taken from material in the Club Archives.

Front and back covers: renderings of Clubhouse facades by architect Thomas Harlan Ellett.
Diana by Ben Cohen: page vi.
Ethel Phelps Stokes Hoyt by Histed: 2.
Mary Schwarz by member Dos Pierson: 4.
Suffrage parade by Dos Pierson: 6.
Reception Room by Kenneth Clark: 8.
Interior courtyard by Kenneth Clark: 14.
Caryatid decor of Allyn Cox by member Elizabeth Elliott: 18.
Clubhouse under construction by Albert Rothschild: 20.
Havemeyer stable by Albert Rothschild: 21.
Longitudinal section of the Clubhouse buildings, courtesy of *American Architect*, May 1933: 24–25.
Private Dining Room by Samuel H. Gottscho, courtesy of the Museum of the City of New York: 26.
Chair from Private Dining Room by Samuel H. Gottscho, courtesy of *House Beautiful*, June 1933: 26.
Library by Samuel H. Gottscho, courtesy of Jane Bigelow Ellett: 27.
Margot Morrow and Mary Villard by Dos Pierson: 28.
Harlequins and clowns, and Josephine Hendrick as *George Washington before the Battle of Trenton*, by member Mary Marvin Breckinridge: 31.
Madame X by Mary Marvin Breckinridge, courtesy of Louise Meière Dunn: 31.
Mannequins in War Relief Workroom by Standard Flashlight Company: 32.
Eleanor Roosevelt and others by Dr. A. David Gurewitsch, courtesy of Edna Perkel Gurewitsch: 34.
Watercolor by Helen Hokinson photographed by Ben Cohen: 36.
New Yorker cover by Mary Petty of May 24, 1941, courtesy of the *New Yorker*: 37.
Mary Schwarz and Emily Belt in "New York Stage Revisited" by Paul Cordes: 41.
Signing of union contract by Standard Flashlight Company: 42.
Club members at Cleveland Museum of Art by member Elsie Wheeler: 49.
The Chocolate Soldier by member Hilda Bijur: 50.
Fire at the Clubhouse by Vincent S. Villard, husband of a member: 50.
Louisa Harris as Pegasus by O. E. Nelson: 52.
"Ballad of the Cos Club" by Standard Flashlight Company: 54.
Isabel Van Dine and Linda Storrow at a fashion show by member Glynne Robinson Betts: 55.
The Loggia by Samuel H. Gottscho: 60.
Arts and Interests Committee meeting by member Caroline Brown: 65.
Annual Meeting, 2008, by Matthew Mauro: 66.
Original cartoon by Helen Hokinson photographed by Ben Cohen: 102.
Board of Governors 2008–2009 by Matthew Mauro: 103.
Presidents Emeritae by Sidney Stafford: 104.
The staff of the Cosmopolitan Club by Matthew Mauro: 106.
Entrance hall by Samuel H. Gottscho: 110.